$$01001101_2$$

128 64 32 16 8 4 2 1

64 + 8 + 4 + 1 = 7

The world of programming brought to life before your eyes!

Computers Illustrated

The Full-Color Guide
To How It All Works

que ®

Computers Illustrated shows you in full color:

- What happens when you turn on your PC

- How your machine loads and runs programs

- Where the information goes that you type in

- How monitors, printers, and modems work

- What goes on within the operating system

Upgrading Your PC Illustrated shows you in full color:

- How to upgrade a computer's processor and memory

- What's needed to install a disk drive, modem, or sound card

- How to add a mouse, printer, game port, or video system

- How DOS, Windows, OS/2, and Mac programming differ

- What loops, clauses, and instructions are

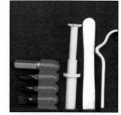

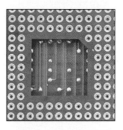

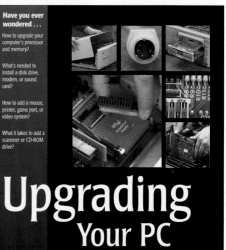

Upgrading
Your PC
Illustrated

que ®

The Full-Color Guide
To How It All Works

PROGRAMMING ILLUSTRATED

Written by
D.F. Scott

Designed by
Amy Peppler-Adams

PROGRAMMING ILLUSTRATED

Library of Congress Catalog No.: 94-65333

ISBN: 1-56529-675-3

97 96 95 94   4 3 2 1

Interpretation of the printing code: the rightmost double-digit number is the year of the book's printing; the rightmost single-digit number, the number of the book's printing. For example, a printing code of 94-1 shows that the first printing of the book occurred in 1994.

Publisher: David P. Ewing

Associate Publisher: Michael Miller

Publishing Director: Joseph Wikert

Managing Editor: Michael Cunningham

Product Marketing Director: Greg Wiegand

Composed in *New Baskerville* and *MCPdigital* by Que Corporation.

CREDITS

Publishing Manager
Brad R. Koch

Acquisitions Editor
Joseph Wikert

Product Director
Bryan Gambrel

Production Editors
Lori Cates
Mike LaBonne

Technical Editor
Paul Logston

Cover Designers
Dan Armstrong
Amy Peppler-Adams

Illustrators
Michael Buck
David Cripe
Dennis Ladigo
Shelly Norris
Anthony StuART

Illustration Art Director
Rich Whitney

Graphic Image Specialists
Teresa Forrester
Tim Montgomery
Dennis Sheehan
Sue VandeWalle

Production Team
Jeff Baker
Angela Bannan
Claudia Bell
Cameron Booker
Jeannie Clark
Anne Dickerson
Karen Dodson
Joelynn Gifford
Michael Hughes
Bob LaRoche
Jay Lesandrini
Beth Lewis
Andrea Marcum
Nanci Sears Perry
Caroline Roop
Amy L. Steed
Becky Tapley
Michael Thomas
Mary Beth Wakefield
Kelli Widdifield

DEDICATION

To my sweet lady Jennifer, who has given me such new and wonderful things to see, to believe in, and to aim for.

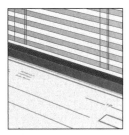

ABOUT THE AUTHOR

D. F. Scott is an independent technical author, artist, musician, and poet. He was technical editor of *The Computer Street Journal*, contributing editor of *ANALOG Computing* and *ST-Log* magazines, and a contributor to *Computer Monthly*. His insights and observations on alternative computing appeared in *Computer Shopper* from 1985 to 1990, during which time he also served as moderator of the *Computer Shopper Information Exchange*. He is the author of *Visual Basic for MS-DOS By Example* from Que, *Extending Visual Basic for Windows* from Sams Publishing, and *Visual Basic for Windows Developer's Guide* from Sams Publishing.

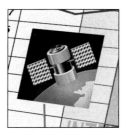

ABOUT THE PRODUCT DIRECTOR

Bryan Gambrel worked closely with D.F. Scott throughout this project. Bryan's knowledge of the product and his editing, writing, and graphic design skills contributed significantly to the success of this book. Bryan has worked for Que Corporation for nearly two years, specializing in programming and operating system books. As a Product Development Specialist he has contributed to several Que books including *Everyday DOS*. Bryan holds a Bachelor of Arts in English Composition and Political Science from DePauw University, and is a fluent programmer in BASIC, Pascal, and Assembler.

ACKNOWLEDGMENTS

There is something truthful about the adage that a small, well-focused team can execute a job more efficiently and with higher quality in a few months' time than a hundred highly motivated managers locked in a conference room for a year. This book stands as testimony to that statement. This project, although quite out of the ordinary, proceeded more smoothly than any project with which I have been associated.

The key to the efficiency of this project has been Joe Wikert. Joe had the vision for this book and the right plan. He then assembled the right people to execute that plan and achieve that vision. I also thank Bryan Gambrel, Lori Cates, and Mike La Bonne for their superb editorial support. Finally, I give special praise to Amy Peppler-Adams, who designed and layed out these pages.

Many successful people have at least one person who has acted as a positive force in their life. I have been blessed with three: my mother, my father, and my wife. This project has been my first published project that allowed me to express ideas with my drawing pen as well as my writing pen. It is impossible for me to make even the slightest mark on a page or canvas without thanking my mother, who taught me to *see* and to *do* at the same time. She taught me that the difference between an artist and an ordinary person is the ability to *do*. On her massive bookshelf stands a little yellow book that states every step one takes should be in honor of the one who taught him to walk. My father is out there fighting the good fight, letting people know that the path to wellness lies first in responsibility for one's own actions. He continues to carry the world on his shoulders, and in the midst of it all, he can dance and celebrate life.

TRADEMARKS

All terms mentioned in this book that are known to be trademarks or service marks have been appropriately capitalized. Que cannot attest to the accuracy of this information. Use of a term in this book should not be regarded as affecting the validity of any trademark or service mark.

ILLUSTRATIONS

The illustrations and color renderings in this book were produced by Erin Brown, David Cripe, Chris Glaser, Dennis Ladigo, Anthony StuART, Craig Thurmond, and Rich Whitney of Accent Technical Communications, an Indianapolis-based company.

Accent's staff of 45 professionals includes illustrators, writers, page composers, programmers, and engineers who use powerful computers and software to produce high-quality text and graphics for printed publications.

Other communication services offered by Accent include computer animation, interactive multimedia presentations, database publishing of industrial catalogs, and CD-ROM production.

WE'D LIKE TO HEAR FROM YOU!

In a continuing effort to produce the highest-quality books possible, Que would like to hear your comments. Let us know what you like and dislike about this book and what we can do to improve it and future Que books.

To provide the most service to you, Prentice Hall Computer Publishing now has a forum on CompuServe (type **GO QUEBOOKS** at any prompt) through which our staff and authors are available for questions and comments. In addition to visiting our forum, feel free to contact me personally on CompuServe at 70714,1516. Or send your comments, ideas, or corrections to me by fax at (317) 581-4663, or write to me at the address below. Your comments will help us to continue publishing the best books on the market.

Bryan Gambrel
Product Development Specialist
Que
201 W. 103rd St.
Indianapolis, IN 46290

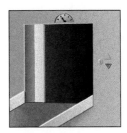

CONTENTS AT A GLANCE

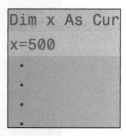

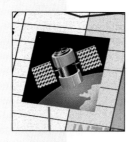

TABLE OF CONTENTS

INTRODUCTION

In Programming Illustrated, you go behind the scenes of your computer, on a guided visual tour of your favorite software applications. Besides seeing how these applications were designed, you also see how they work with your computer, operating system, operating environment, and with other applications.

This book takes you on a guided visual tour of some of the most popular types of software applications, and shows their major components. You also see how the application was built and how it controls the components of your computer. You see the complete process the programmer went through to design and build the application.

This book also takes you on a guided tour through several programming languages and discusses the capabilities and uses of each language. The tour may help you decide whether you want to attempt programming, and which language is best for you to start with.

You learn how to design your programs by following the process an application designer/ programmer goes through. This book shows you how successful commercial applications and computer programs are designed, rather than teaching you how to write a program.

The 13 chapters of text and 65 four-color spreads in this book take the abstract concepts and images of programming and make them easier to understand. The full-color drawings present unique compilations of everyday objects and examples that reduce the complex concept of application design to a simple level of understanding.

What this book attempts to do is draw a holistic picture of the programming process. You see what goes on in the mind of a programmer during the course of everyday work. Along the way, you may discover that programming is not such a complex process, once the layer of abstraction has been removed. Who knows, you may even find that you want to learn how to design and build programs yourself!

CHAPTER 1

AN APPLICATION IS A MACHINE

A computer programmer is like a mechanical engineer. A mechanical engineer assembles parts into machines that perform work. A programmer builds computer programs that provide solutions to problems. A mechanical engineer uses wheels and gears to build his machines. A programmer uses statements and formulas—words and numbers—to build his programs.

The world of computer programs can be divided into system programs (they make your computer run), utility programs (they help you maintain your system and back up your work), and application programs (they help you perform tasks such as analyzing stock data, writing a report, or creating a presentation). This book focuses primarily on application programs.

As the preceding definition suggests, an application is an advanced program used in a business setting for multiple tasks. Examples of applications include Word processors (such as WordPerfect and Microsoft Word), spreadsheets (such as Lotus 1-2-3 and Excel), database managers (such as dBASE and Paradox), portfolio trackers (such as CA—Simply Money and Quicken), graphics developers (such as PageMaker and CorelDRAW!), and accounting systems (such as QuickBooks and Microsoft Money). What makes an application unique among program categories is that the application's users may shape the program to work as they see fit.

An application is like a machine. You may remember from high school science that a machine performs a measurable amount of work proportional to the amount of energy applied. For example, an automobile engine takes energy (gasoline) and performs work (propels the car). An application works much the same way: it takes the user's input (keystrokes) and produces work (a word processing document, spreadsheet, and so on).

Also like a machine, the language used to write an application has parts that work together similar to gears, wheels, and levers. Combined in just the right way, they perform a measurable amount of work. The results of the application—its output data—relate directly and proportionally to its input data. For example, a word processing document is a product of its raw text, a spreadsheet projection is a product of its numbers, and a report is a product of its database.

AN APPLICATION PERFORMS WORK

I f you've ever had an erector set, you'll remember the joy of assembling gears, wheels, and levers, applying power, and watching in awe as everything worked. Programming is like working with an erector set: A programmer assembles components, applies power to them, and sees whether they work.

Following the erector set example, the sketch in this section shows a group of devices that symbolize some of the inner workings of a modern application. The application begins at the top left, where the user enters data (a number) into one of the cells of a spreadsheet. The application processes that data as a user event. In this sketch, the user event (symbolized as a red marble) flows through a pipe and drops into a sort of Ferris wheel, which represents the buffer. The buffer is a temporary storage area where events are kept until they can be processed. Although events may happen quickly, they are stored in the buffer and released at timed intervals, which are determined by the speed of the user's computer and designated within the program.

This buffer wheel (along with the entire application) is driven by a large, rotating power source labeled *main*. Most programming languages (especially C and C++) employ some form of "main element" to control which component of the application is activated at what time. A large wheel was chosen to represent main because the main module defines the cycle of a program. The main module directs and controls the entire application by determining which routines operate at what time. Routines control such real-world processes as clearing the screen, reading data, and writing to the screen. The rest of the sketch consists of the gears and levers branching off the main power source, which represent the routines that carry out the actual work of main.

From the buffer, the event marble flows to the "merry-go-round" labeled *loop clause*. That gear, along with the gears labeled *calculations* and *macro*, are the number-crunching elements—the formulas and macros—that actually carry out the work for main.

The event marble then moves to the stack, which is a memory device. In this sketch, the stack is represented as a belt-driven elevator. The event waits on the stack to be processed by the logic components, which are represented by the plumbing pipes that "magically" recompose the user event into a data product (labeled *output*) that the program can actually use. The "magic" that finally transforms the raw data into the final output is determined by the formulas and macros of the number-crunching gears. The box (output) represents the final product. For the sake of this spreadsheet, the contents of the "Quarterly Totals" cell would contain this output.

Now let's look at a real-world example. Suppose that you have a spreadsheet that calculates the annual sales forecast for your company based on weekly sales reports. You must type in the weekly sales data (the event marbles). The buffer holds these weekly sales figures in memory until the program is ready to calculate them. The weekly sales figures are passed on to the number-crunching section, where they are measured, added together, and averaged out. The program then places each of the weekly sales figures in the stack until all of the sales figures are received. After all the relevant data is processed, the data transformation takes place—and your result, the annual sales forecast, is the blue box.

LOGIC

OUTPUT

STACK

MACRO

CALCULATIONS

MAIN

LOOP CLAUSE

THE APPLICATION MODEL

An application, as defined earlier, is a specific type of computer program. About half of the programs sold today qualify as applications; the other half are games and simulations. Although the overall nature of the application's work is defined by the programmer (for example, does it save data as sentences and paragraphs, or as rows and columns?), it is the user who defines the specific job that an application will perform (such as writing a letter or a newsletter, producing a budget, or balancing a checkbook).

The programmer of a modern graphical (Windows) application can spend more time concentrating on the application's specific task because most of the small, common details can be handled by the many "support" layers that work "beneath" the application—generally by the operating system (such as DOS) and the operating environment (such as Microsoft Windows).

The operating system acts as an interface between the computer and programs; DOS is what makes all IBM-compatible machines "understand" the same programs and applications. The operating environment provides the graphical interface; Windows

allows programs to have the same look and feel—and understand mouse movements. The programmer does not need to worry about each individual application gathering user input from the keyboard or the mouse, sending characters of data to the hard drive, and displaying output in a new window; DOS and Windows provide common ways of doing these things.

Because DOS and Windows are also programs, the computer must devote as much time to them as is necessary. As a result, the programmer is freed from total responsibility for the smaller details. Before the standard Microsoft Windows graphical environment, however, the programmer had to concentrate on such matters as "where's the arrow?" and "how grey is my button?"

The structure of an application is divided into six categories, shown here as slices in a pie chart. The pie is divided into two halves, the left half of which is devoted to the mathematics and number-crunching portion of the application, the right half to

Arithmeti

Data Manipulation

Recipe

Directions

Data Entry

Display

Directions is the most important slice on the right side. Directions are the commands a user gives the application—such as the specific instructions or commands pulled down from the menu bar in a spreadsheet application. Data entry, by contrast, is the delivery of processable data to the application. A user typing into a word processor, or the interpretation of a stored file after it has been retrieved, qualifies as data entry. Finally, the display slice covers all the text and graphics that are shown by the application. Displaying the results of the application falls into this category, because an application can theoretically work without actually showing the fruits of its labor to the user (besides, the user does not need to see the result of every intermediate formula and calculation in the stock portfolio application—it would probably only make the application more confusing).

the input/output portion. The height of each slice in the pie chart denotes its importance.

Arithmetic is the most important slice on the left side. An application generally can't do much work if it can't add and subtract. Even a simple text editor needs to be capable of counting how many characters are in a document. The second most important part of an application is data manipulation—which includes the capability to store and retrieve data from both short-term storage (memory) and long-term storage (floppy disks and hard drives). A program is not of much use if it cannot store the data it has calculated.

The last mathematical element on the left side is the recipe. Every program is filled with repetitious tasks, such as searching for a specific file in a hard drive. Just as you look in a cookbook to use the same cake recipe each time, a programmer uses a task's recipe each time the task is needed.

SPOTLIGHT ON
"THE FIRST SPREADSHEET APPLICATION"

Dan Bricklin and Bob Frankston (left to right) may be the creators of the modern application model. Bricklin invented the spreadsheet, and Frankston molded Bricklin's ideas into a marketable product, called VisiCalc. Bricklin's original application, unlike almost any other application developed to that day (1979), paused for user events before starting to process data. The function of the program was also defined by the user, not the programmer. Before Bricklin's and Frankston's work, the function of a program was defined in advance by its programmers. If a program calculated the average speed of an aircraft, for example, that's all it did. Bricklin originally intended to make VisiCalc into a calculating machine rather than an application. Frankston reworked Bricklin's "machine control program" into software, which has been accepted by many as the first modern application program.

What Exactly Does a Programmer Do?

The objective of all programming is to represent a task—real or imaginary—as a logical and mathematical process. The desired task may be completely mathematical such as accounting, geometrical such as floor planning, or recreational such as game playing. Understanding the principles behind the task is the first step to knowing the elements the program must contain. Next, the programmer must create a mathematical and logical model of the task. In other words, the programmer must find a way to describe absolutely every part of the task mathematically and logically.

Everything about a computer is logical and is made up of numbers and formulas. It is therefore relatively easy for a programmer to conceive an accounting application, because the task of accounting is comprised of numbers and formulas. Consider, however, an application that produces floor plans and landscaping maps. Such tasks at first may not seem numerical—but here geometry plays a role. Tasks such as drawing where the trees or shrubbery are to be planted must be simulated with program instructions.

Now consider an application for doctors that generates a list of diagnoses when given a list of symptoms. The part of this application that maintains the lists of symptoms, causes, and medications would be the easiest part to create—this would be the database manager (part of the data manipulation slice from the previous page). A database is a collection of organized data (such as a doctor's list of patients). The database manager is the segment of the application that controls the contents of the database (the data lists).

It's certainly far more difficult for the programmer to simulate the decision-making task than to maintain the lists of symptoms and medications. Unless the programmer is a medical doctor, he would need to do extensive research and interviews to fully understand the doctor's decision-making process—almost as if he were a medical student. In addition to using academic knowledge, a doctor must rely to some degree on gut feelings and intuition when making a clinical diagnosis. Therefore, the programmer must create an application that simulates a doctor's intuition. Although creating a program that simulates the doctor's intuition is probably not possible, an application can be created that simulates just the factual functions, leaving the intuition to the doctor running the application.

When modeling a task that would otherwise be performed by a person, the programmer must thoroughly comprehend the fundamentals of the work and the principles, laws, and mathematics governing it. The programmer does not have to master the task; for example, the programmer in the earlier example (the medical diagnosis application) need not be a medical doctor. He must understand the job of a medical doctor only to the degree that the doctors won't be insulted, aggravated, or confused while using this application.

THE FUNDAMENTAL TOOLS OF A PROGRAMMER

It is not necessary for a computer to have the actual programming language on its hard drive in order to run an application written in that language. In fact, most programmers know multiple languages, and often use more than one language to write a single application.

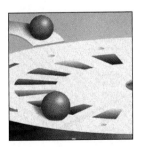

A programming language is merely an intermediary between the programmer and a machine. All programming languages merely translate the programmer's code into the computer's native language. This native language, at its core, is comprised of binary digits (1s and 0s), which are far more difficult for the human programmer to manipulate than the English-like programming language phrases.

The written text of a program is called its *source code.* This code consists of instructions—such as a list of things to do today—which are performed in sequence. This sequence is not necessarily top-to-bottom or beginning-to-end, but there is a sequence, nonetheless. Certain programming languages that have a greater resemblance to ordinary English written language are called *high-level* languages. BASIC, Pascal, C, C++, Modula, Ada, PROLOG, COBOL, and FORTRAN are the most common high-level languages in use today. Machine languages and assembly languages are called *low-level* languages because they are considered "closer" to the computer. In most diagrams of computer functions (such as the "monument" shown in "The Application Model"), the functions toward the bottom are those that pertain more to the operation of the computer, whereas those toward the top pertain more to people, or to the user's specified task.

A programmer uses a compiler to write programs. The compiler has a screen that resembles a word processor, into which the programmer types the high-level instructions. Then the compiler translates the programmer's high-level instructions into low-level code that the computer can understand and run—namely, object code. The compiler generates a file that contains an application's object code.

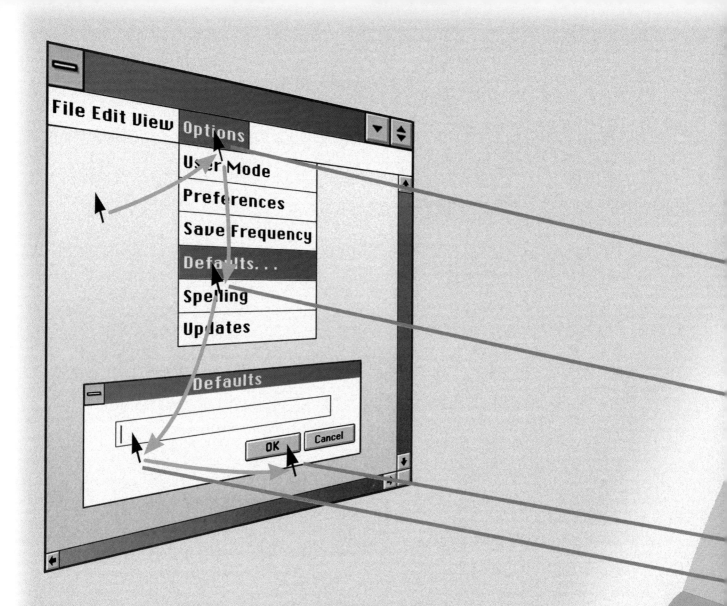

HOW A PROGRAM COMMUNICATES WITH PEOPLE

In this diagram, the mouse movements show a series of user input events (remember the red marbles from "A Program Performs Work?"). The lines leading from the mouse pointers show each event's relation to the computer's internal tasks. In the preceding section, you read about the distinction between high- and low-level tasks. In the model shown here, computer tasks are portrayed as layers of a bisected sphere—similar to the familiar cutaway view of the Earth. Here, the core represents the low-level tasks—generally the Basic Input/Output System (BIOS) or its equivalent, which handles the operations of the computer's hardware (the printer, the monitor, and so on).

**OPERATING
ENVIRONMENT**

**OPERATING
SYSTEM**

In this drawing, you can imagine the user moving the pointer arrow with the mouse up to the Options menu, pulling it down to reveal the Defaults option (the Direction task), which brings up the Defaults dialog box. The arrow is then used to click on the text box—so that the user can enter text (the Data Entry task)—and then is moved over to the OK button. This sequence contains four major user events. The Options menu and Defaults command are both provided by the operating environment (Windows). The Defaults dialog box is a service of the application framework—a resource provided by the specific compiler the programmer used (such as Visual Basic, Turbo Pascal, or Borland C++). Clicking the OK button passes the command through to the lowest level—the operating system itself. Commands that affect the operating state of the computer, such as starting a new application, are always passed to the operating system.

CORE
BIOS

HOW A PROGRAM COMMUNICATES WITH OTHER PROGRAMS

Today's applications need to be concerned with the likelihood of other applications using computer memory at the same time. Modern operating environments, such as Microsoft Windows and IBM's OS/2, allow programs to not run simultaneously, but also to share data. A system in which multiple programs can run at the same time and share the same data is called a *multitasking system.*

It is possible (and often common) for a user to have as many as a dozen applications running in the operating environment at one time; for the sake of simplicity, however, we use only three applications in our models. Marbles 1, 2, and 3 represent the three programs, each running independently of the operating system/environment represented by the OS marble. Imagine marbles 1, 2, and 3 as though they were along the rim of a clock. The OS marble is like the motor controlling the sweeping second hand of a clock, which points to, or "recognizes," each of the marbles in turn, one at a time.

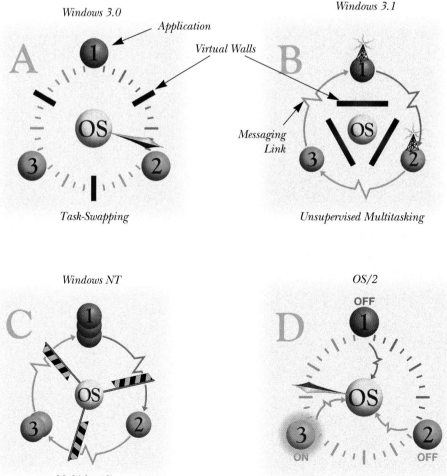

Windows 3.0

A — *Application* — *Virtual Walls*

Task-Swapping

Windows 3.1

B — *Messaging Link*

Unsupervised Multitasking

Windows NT

C

Multithreading

OS/2

D — OFF — ON — OFF

Supervised Multitasking

Panel A shows the nearly obsolete design used in Windows 3.0. As you can see, the separate applications are each given an equal share of the operating system's time. The individual applications are also not allowed to communicate with one another —virtual walls built between the applications bar them from communicating except directly through the OS. Because the applications are not aware that other applications exist, this cannot truly be called "multitasking;" the OS instead swaps from one application to another, without the applications being aware. It's like breaking up one big computer into three smaller ones. Because of the rigid division of time for each application, this method is called *task-swapping*.

Panel B depicts the multitasking used in Windows 3.1. Here, the individual programs have direct communication with other applications, but have no direct communication with the operating system or environment (the virtual walls are used to block communication between the OS and applications). Instead, when a program wants data belonging to another program, it broadcasts a "public" message requesting that information. Another program may respond by attempting to retrieve this data on behalf of the broadcaster. When this happens, a data transaction takes place; the broadcasting application is the *client* and the responding application is the *server*.

In this design, control passes from program 1 to program 2 to program 3, but it is up to the programs themselves to pass control on to the next program. This means the programmer may have to keep track of when his application can reasonably consider itself "done for the moment." Otherwise, the next application may wait in line forever (and its user along with it). This is a cooperative multitasking design, because the applications must themselves decide when to turn over control to the next application requesting control.

Panel C portrays the design in place in Microsoft Windows NT. This operating system is capable of multithreading—running tasks within multiple applications concurrently. Rather than perform the instructions from application 1 (1, 2, 3 ...) first, and

then perform the instructions from application 2 (100, 101, 102 ...), and so on, a multithreading environment can run the applications at nearly the same time: 1, 100, 2, 101, 3, 102, and so on.

The operating system oversees the distribution of control, and may temporarily prevent the next program from receiving control prematurely by throwing down what is called a *semaphore*, shown here as yellow-and-black blockade gates.

Panel D shows the design used by IBM's OS/2. The OS distributes equal amounts of execution time to each application (similar to the task-swapping of Windows 3.0), and suspends the nonrunning programs. When a suspended program is reawakened, it may either continue execution as though nothing happened, or monitor exactly how long it was asleep and compensate by making up for lost time.

Finally, Panel E depicts the complex design of recent versions of UNIX, similar to the multithreading of Windows NT. UNIX has always been capable of temporarily opening separate copies of running applications, so that one important task belonging to the application doesn't wait for another task to complete before it begins. The UNIX design distributes equal timeslices to each application, and then periodically adjusts the times as needed. In fact, a new process literally negotiates with UNIX for a desired slice of time. UNIX considers the request and gives out the time it sees fit.

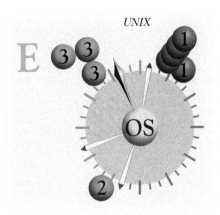

Scheduled Multitasking

THE WORK PRODUCT
OF THE APPLICATION

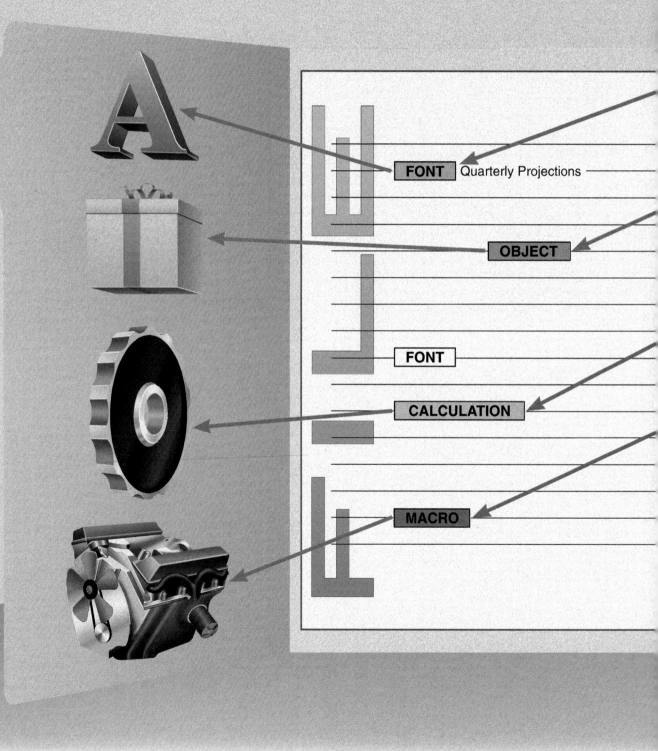

DOCUMENT MATRIX

File Options Windows Help

Quarterly Projections

During the run time of an application, a collection of data is formed, called the *document*. This data may be in the form of a table, a letter, or a full-scale database. Before it becomes a stored file on disk (and even after), it resides in memory as the document.

Modern operating environments make it possible for a document to borrow resources from other files, from parts of the operating environment itself, or from other documents. Here, we show a document in two forms: At right, as the ongoing product (a presentation) being generated by the user; and to the left of that, in the document's final, stored form—as a file. A stored file may contain "pointers" to external resources, shown to the far left. These pointers act as the computer equivalent of those reference marks you find in encyclopedia entries, such as, "See *Indiana* for

more information." With modern applications, it is not necessary to reproduce the same data for multiple documents—you can reference the file in which it is saved. This is just one reason among many why it is just as important for the programmer to design the data as well as the final application.

On the left side of the drawing, we have chosen a cog to represent a calculation because, although a calculation plays a great part in the number-crunching sequences, it is driven by the main module and cannot move on its own. An engine was chosen to represent a macro because a macro has its own engine and can run outside of the main function. But of the external resources shown here, the object (the pink package) is perhaps most important, because it represents a standardized way for one application to present data to another. Objects are discussed further in Chapter 2.

CHAPTER 2

THE ROLE OF
LANGUAGE

Just as you use English every day to communicate with other people, a computer programmer uses one of several programming languages every day to communicate. At first, you would think that a programming language is used as a means for the programmer to communicate with the computer—such as presenting a list of things to do, or a series of instructions (representing *Directions* and *Recipe*, respectively, from "The Application Model" in Chapter 1). Actually, a programming language, like any other written language (such as English), conveys a message between people, only indirectly.

The programmer of an application is really telling the computer how to respond to the *user* of that application. The application gives the user a forum for communicating with the programmer (such as a blank word processing document). The application contains all the instructions necessary for it to process the user's response (input—characters and numbers) and use that input to generate new information for the user (output—a report or letter). Yet the application is nearly useless unless the application accepts a wide range of possible responses. The fewer commands the application understands, the less the application is capable of doing.

So an application acts as a conveyor of *dialogue* between the programmer and the user. Imagine writing a stage play with two characters—but you know only what one of them will be saying. You write character #1's opening monologue, but you cannot write character #2's response. Because you do not know what character #2 will be talking about, you must write several different responses for character #1. In other words, you can write only character #1's opening monologue and a set of possible responses to character #2. To some extent, this is what writing an application is like.

TRANSLATING ENGLISH INTO AN APPLICATION

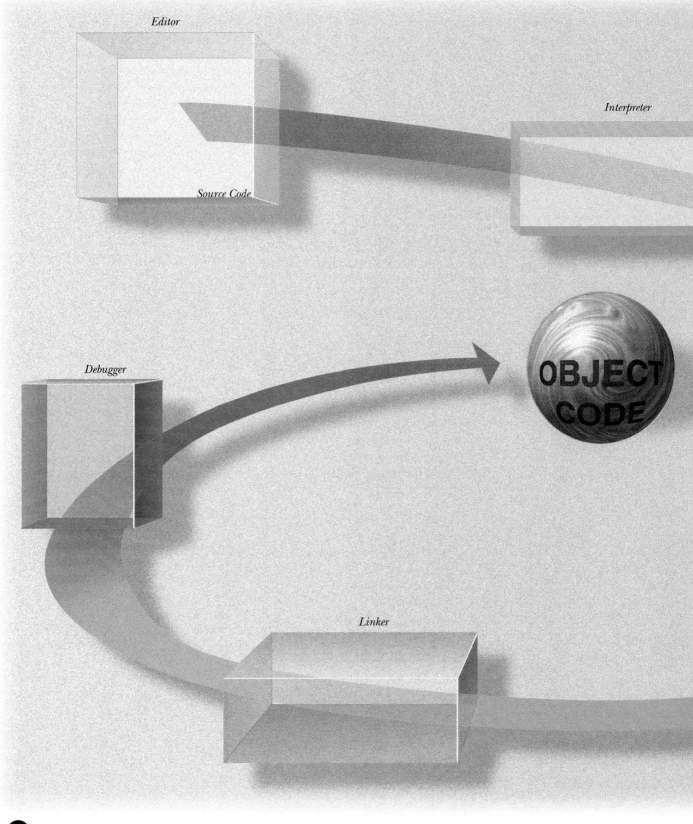

When creating an application (changing the programmer's ideas from English-like instructions called *source code* into the object code a computer can run), a programmer might use as many as six different programs. The programming process begins within the *editor* program (such as the DOS Editor or another text editor), in which the programmer types the program.

An *interpreter* program simulates running a program line-by-line, without actually translating the program into object code the computer can understand. You can compare the action of an interpreter to that of a person reading a book written in French and translating it line-by-line into English as he reads it. A programmer might use an interpreter to test how specific sections of a program work before compiling the entire program into stand-alone object code. In other cases, such as QBasic programs, the application is intentionally left to run under an interpreter—no object code is ever created. To run such an application, the user must start it from within the interpreter (QBasic, in this case).

The *compiler* is the most important tool used by most programmers. The compiler interprets the entire source code as a package (not line-by-line) and saves the newly interpreted code as an object code file that can be run at any time. Unlike an interpreter, the compiler does not need to reinterpret the source code each time the application is run. Although a compiler generally does not produce the finished application, it is capable of triggering other programs that

do put the finishing touches on an application. If you used the Turbo C++ compiler to create your application, your application is translated into object code that can be run by using any computer, whether or not it has the compiler.

The *assembler* is the primary tool of assembly language programmers. The source code of an assembly language program is very similar to the object code. In fact, they are so similar that the source code directly corresponds to object code *without* having to be interpreted. Assembly language is very similar to machine language (which is the computer's native language).

Most professional applications usually consist of more than one piece of object code, compiled separately, yet *linked* together before execution. These pieces may provide such ordinary and useful resources as opening a text file or displaying text on-screen.

Compiler

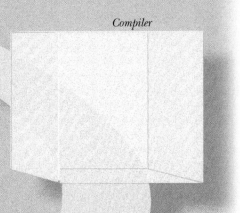

The linker attaches these separate blocks of code to the assembled program.

Debugger programs allow the programmer to see inside the application as it runs. Think of the debugger as an X-ray machine in a doctor's office. The debugger monitors not only the state of the program, but also the state of the computer. This way, if the running program "crashes" or otherwise does something the programmer doesn't expect, the debugger may provide some clues as to why this is happening.

Assembler

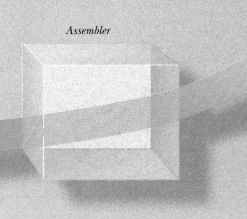

THE SEQUENCE OF INSTRUCTIONS

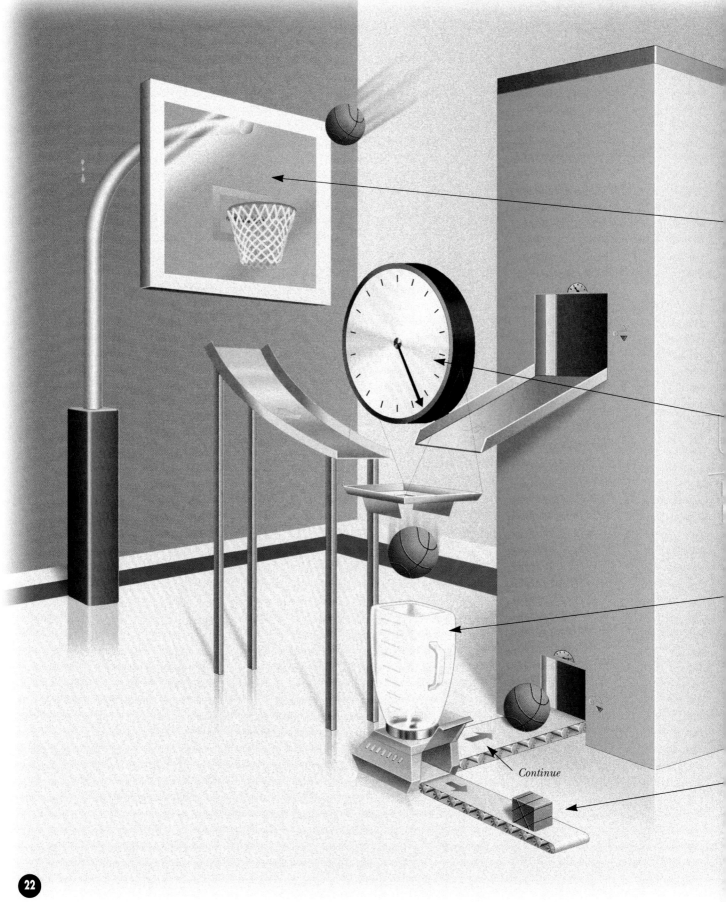

Continue

*M*odular programming is the most common and versatile programming. The source code of a modular application can be broken into many smaller chunks of source code. Just as an automobile is built as several separate parts (tires, frame, and engine) and then assembled into a car, complex applications can be written as separate modules and then assembled into a complex application. To demonstrate this point, the drawing shows five everyday objects that represent the five common components of an ordinary module.

Header

Loop Clause

Conditional Test

Processing

Output

In C++, modern Pascal, Modula-2, and most modern versions of BASIC, a module begins with a single line of text (the *parameter line*) that lists the items with which the module will be concerned. For instance, if a module is to search for a particular word in a block of text, the parameter line would tell the module that it will receive a word to look for, and a block of text to search. The module is said to receive these two items as *input parameters*.

A basketball hoop receives a ball each day as its input parameter, so this hoop represents the part of each module that *receives* input. Naturally, the big, orange balls represent the input itself. After the hoop receives the input, a chute directs the bucketed ball through to a grocer's scale, which represents the part of the module that *tests*, or "weighs," the input.

After the ball is weighed (and we know more about the input now than we did before), the scale drops the ball into the waiting blender. Using the input as its main ingredient, this blender—which represents the math calculations within a module—attempts to change the input into something suitable for output. The objective of the module is to create at least one new and useful output value from its input. For example, such an output value might identify the location of a word in a block of text. The new output value shown here, being pushed out of the blender, is a green, square basketball.

Sometimes the process of testing and evaluating has to be repeated multiple times within a module before a desired output value is found. For instance, a module might try several locations before it finds a particular word in a block of text. This drawing uses an elevator to take the incomplete data from the blender back up to the grocer's scale. This process repeats as many times as necessary.

FINDING ORDER IN MODULES

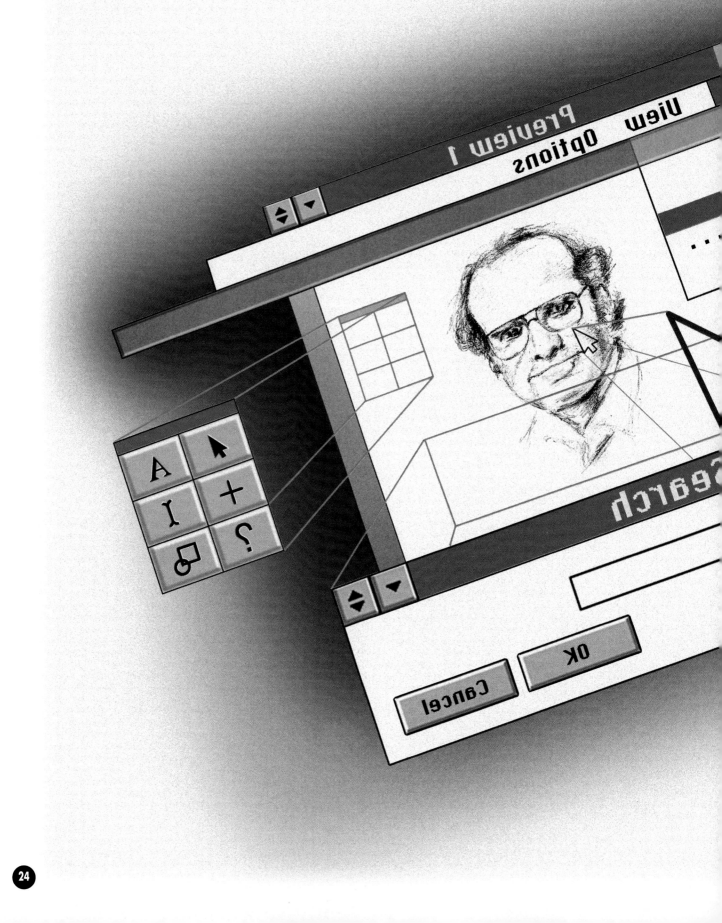

Most applications sold today are graphical applications: They're operated with a mouse, and use menu bars and *dialog panels* (also known as *dialog boxes*). In the source code of an application, you'll find that the business of a dialog panel is generally handled by a single module. When the user clicks on a menu command such as Edit Search, he triggers a process within a module that brings up the Search dialog panel.

The purpose of such a panel is to ask for text from the user, start the search, and report the status of that search to the user. The search process is generally another module that accepts the text from the dialog panel module and reports back to that dialog panel (not the user).

What part of the application brings up the Search dialog panel? The menu bar is generally a service provided to the programmer by the operating environment (such as Windows, OS/2 PM, Apple Finder, or Motif), although in its compiled form it's really just another module. Toolbars and tool boxes like those you see here are resources that the compiler package (such as Turbo C++) helps the programmer construct, although in their compiled forms they, too, are modules.

In Chapter 1, you saw that the graphical components of an application are Directions, Data Entry, and Display. Menu bars and toolbars are each components of the Directions section. By contrast, the primary user input—the typing of text, drawing of pictures, and the like—are the Data Entry components. They, too, are handled by way of modules. One such module might be triggered by keyboard input—changing the font of the current character by looking it up in the font table that corresponds with the new font selected by the user.

The point of all this is that modules receive input data from the body of the application that calls them, and pass output data back to that body. The display-oriented modules (such as the menu bar and toolbar) direct the user data through to the arithmetic modules deeper in the system. The arithmetic modules "convert" this data and pass it back to the display modules, which in turn present it to the user.

The Making of an Application

When you see a book that contains the text of a program, what you're really looking at is the source code of that program. The computer cannot read the source code; that is why a program must be interpreted, compiled, assembled, and linked. The source code describes a program to the human beings who are reading it. The computer can understand only the object code of a program (after it has been interpreted, compiled, assembled, and linked). When you look through a directory for an executable program (an EXE file), you're really searching for a file that contains the object code of that program.

In "Translating English into an Application," you saw the steps taken when converting source code into object code. How does a professional programmer convey ideas as source code? Certainly there are a number of different techniques used by programmers; modular programming, however, has brought some standardization—and with it some common ways for programmers to work.

A professional programmer first makes the program perform its primary functions. When building a word processor, the programmer first needs to build the elements that manage the characters and numbers. The engine, in other words, is built first. One such module belonging to the engine might delete a character to the left of the cursor. Another such module might locate the cursor. Because these features are modularized, the programmer is free to create them one at a time, making one module work before proceeding to the next.

Once the engine is working, the programmer can then begin implementing the framework—the input and output features. One module in the framework monitors the status of the keyboard, waiting for a "user

SPOTLIGHT ON NIKLAUS WIRTH

Professor Niklaus Wirth created the Pascal programming language and its successor, Modula-2. Introduced in 1971, the Pascal language (named for French mathematician Blaise Pascal) is credited with being the first truly modular high-level programming language; C was to come later. This development was by no means accidental; Professor Wirth designed Pascal as a language to teach the proper concepts of programming—using modules. In his 1971 paper "Program Development by Stepwise Refinement," Wirth proposed two major improvements to high-level program design. The first—the use of separate modules with simplified, standardized structures—is demonstrated here. The second is that the make-up of a program is defined by the data it produces, not vice versa.

event" (shown in "The Computer Is a Machine" in Chapter 1). This module might check to see whether the key that was pressed is "Delete" and, if so, start the character-deletion module that's already a part of the engine. When the character-deletion module is finished, the engine then signals for the cursor to be repositioned. The working cursor location module within the engine is run. You can easily see why the engine components are made to work first; otherwise, how will the programmer know whether the messages passed by the framework modules are received and understood?

The principle that Professor Niklaus Wirth demonstrated is really no more difficult than what we find today in our abundance of self-help guides: The best way to approach a difficult task is by breaking it into smaller, simpler parts.

WHY USE AN INTERPRETER?

A high-level language interpreter executes instructions one at a time as it reads them.

Some C++ compiler packages include interpreters as a way to test segments of the source code before compiling the entire program.

Some BASIC language packages, however, such as Microsoft Visual Basic for Windows, are interpreters only; they don't produce

truly compiled standalone code. Why? The BASIC programming language was designed to be graspable at once by the beginning programmer. The fact that BASIC is largely an interpreted language means the programmer can make changes and run those changes now, rather than wait until the long compilation process is over. The trade-off is that interpreted language code runs far more slowly than compiled object code. As a natural progression, after a programmer becomes proficient with BASIC, he usually proceeds to a lower-level language, such as C++.

WHY USE AN ASSEMBLER?

You will remember from before that the source code for a compiler does not directly correspond to the object code understood by the machine; it must be assembled and linked. The compiler has to interpret the instructions in the source code and figure out a way to say them in the object code that the computer will understand. Often, the compiler does not pick the most efficient way of telling the machine what to do. Writing in assembly language, the programmer can control exactly what instructions are placed in the object code. Thus, the programmer can make a program as efficient as possible without the additional layers of high-level code.

WHAT IT MEANS TO BE OBJECT-ORIENTED

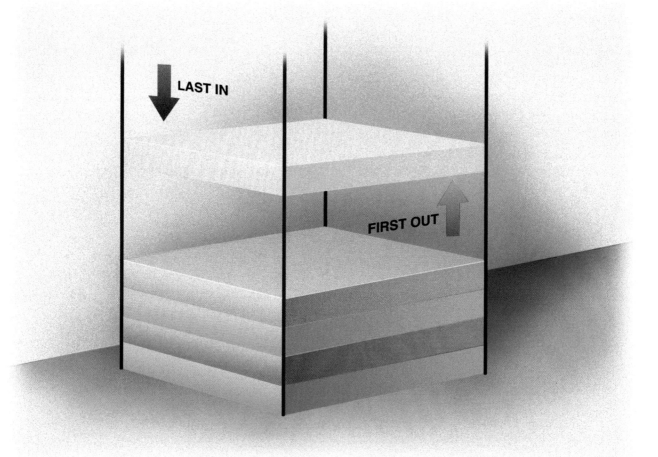

The second of Professor Niklaus Wirth's primary principles of programming says that the data truly defines the application. Modern applications that inhabit a multitasking operating environment are designed to be object-oriented. In other words, the data an application produces is designed to be accessed by this and other applications, in a standardized format.

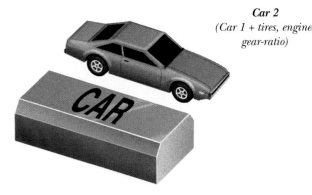

Car 1
(12 feet long, 8 feet wide, red)

Car 2
(Car 1 + tires, engine gear-ratio)

Balloon 1
*(globular, made of plastic,
filled with air, floats upward)*

Balloon 2
*(Balloon 1 + gas furnace,
wicker basket)*

Programmers write an application so that it can read blocks of data, as long as they fit the desired qualifications. A powerful word processor such as Word for Windows can accept objects of several types (such as blocks of text, drawings, and segments of spreadsheets) as long as they fit the specific characteristics. It would be nearly impossible for the programmer to write code modules instructing the application how to interpret and handle every possible object. Instead, the application handles groups of similar objects in a like manner. All of the data is stored as a generic object in the computer's memory.

If a friend asked you to describe a balloon to her, and you didn't know whether she meant a helium balloon or a hot-air balloon, you might say that a balloon has the following characteristics: (*globular, made of plastic, filled with air, floats upward*). This definition gives your friend enough information to envision a balloon, but is general enough to cover both a helium balloon and a hot-air balloon. To describe the hot-air balloon specifically, you might add the following characteristics to your definition of a balloon: (*gas furnace, wicker basket*).

It is easier to write a program dealing with very broadly defined objects, because there are fewer limitations. As you can see here, it would be easier to repair a "car" that has the characteristics (*twelve feet long, eight feet wide, and red*) than a car with the additional characteristics (*tires, engine, and gear-ratio*). The more specifically an object is defined in an application, the more limiting its code is.

THE LEVELS OF PROGRAMMING LANGUAGES

From time to time, this book has used the terms "high-level language" and "low-level language" to describe the differences between programming languages. The lowest level of programming language is machine language. This means exactly what it says: the language of the machine. In its most raw form, machine language is a series of binary digits (1s and 0s, or bits). Theoretically, you could program a computer by using 1s and 0s alone—but you wouldn't want to.

Macro assembly language isn't discussed in this book at great length; however, you need to know what it is in general. In machine language, there are successive patterns of 1s and 0s that each represent instructions to the computer. Assembly language simply replaces those patterns of 1s and 0s with abbreviated terms; they aren't exactly English, but they are at least more readable to the programmer. Assembly language is the most cryptic of the common programming languages discussed in this book.

"High-level" procedural languages are perhaps the most commonly used today, and are the primary subject of this book. C++, C, Pascal, BASIC, Ada, COBOL, FORTRAN, and PROLOG are all high-level procedural languages. We call them "high-level" because their syntaxes use more common mathematical and linguistic symbols, and are more easily read by humans. In turn, this makes these languages more difficult for the computer to interpret; that's why there are compilers and interpreter programs to act as go-betweens.

```
rec   1 first
        middle
        last
      2 city
        state
        zip
```

```
For x=1 to no times
while proj<100
compute dist
wend
next x
```

```
move delay, ax
mov si, ax
shl si, 1
mov ax, si
```

```
11011011
01101100
01011001
10110011
```

One higher level of programming language exists, which uses more graphical elements such as boxes, arrows, and large enclosing brackets. Such graphical elements are used to better show the relationships between elements of data, or the transition or hand-off between modules in an application. For lack of a better term, such languages are called *fourth-generation languages,* or 4GLs. Practice has shown such pictorial languages to be less adaptable to general purposes than standard procedural languages, however; thus, they are seldom used in business today.

APHICAL

OCEDURAL

CRO ASSEMBLY

ACHINE LANGUAGE

Next x

CHAPTER 3

THE PARTS OF SPEECH

All languages have rules. The rules that govern proper English are called grammar. If you don't follow the correct rules when you put together a sentence, no one will understand you. Likewise, if you don't follow the rules that govern a programming language while writing a program, the compiler—and ultimately the computer itself—will not be able to understand your program.

Each programming language has its own set of rules. Just as with spoken and written languages, some programming languages more closely resemble one another. The low-level languages, such as assembly language and machine language, are governed by bits, flags, and options. The high-level languages, such as BASIC and Pascal, were invented to allow the programmer to communicate by using rules with styles and forms more common to people than to the computer. Although sometimes difficult to grasp, the grammar of English is more natural to us than tables of raw mathematical data.

Although English, French, and Spanish all use widely varying words to mean different things, their methods for constructing sentences and phrases are often remarkably similar. Although their location within a sentence differs, the concepts of nouns, verbs, and adjectives, for example, are similar in these three languages. Also in these languages, the specific rules are different, although the basic structures are nearly the same.

C++, BASIC, and Pascal all use widely varying terms and devices to convey instructions, although parts appear to have been borrowed from one another. Programmers who learn how to use these mechanisms with one high-level language should be able to transport this skill nearly intact to another language. This chapter demonstrates those "grammatical" structures that you'll find in the most commonly used high-level programming languages.

```
Dim x As Cur
x=500
    .
    .
    .
    .
```

THE ROLE OF VARIABLES

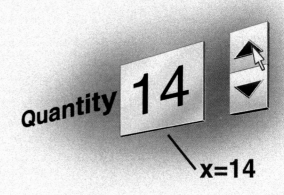

A programmer must write an application to perform actions on an unknown value. Just as you write a check the same way regardless of its value, the programmer of an accounting application must write the built-in formulas without knowing any specific values. The programmer uses *variables* (named for their counterparts in algebra) to represent these unknown values. Just as the values of checks in your checkbook are different, the value (contents) of a variable can be changed.

In high-level languages, as in algebra, variables usually represent numerical values. The most commonly used variable term in algebra is *x*. Fortunately, modern programming languages allow you to use more descriptive variable terms than *x*, such as *num_entries*. Are there more entries in the database than memory can handle at present—say, more than 256? You can test for this condition by comparing the unknown value *x* (or *num_entries*) to 256, which is a known value.

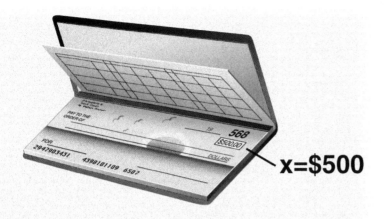

x=$500

Anything that can be counted, measured, or otherwise evaluated can be represented by a variable. Variables do not always have to represent unknown numbers, however. A variable can have a specific purpose in the application in which it is contained, and yet have no bearing on the world at-large. For instance, in a word processor, is Overstrike mode turned on? A variable named *overstrike* might be assigned a 1 for yes, or a 0 for no. This variable only denotes whether the Overstrike key is turned on or off.

Now let's look at a sample code fragment that uses variables. Variable *x* plays three roles in this modern BASIC module. In the sketch, it first appears on the Definition line at the top; this line tells the Visual Basic interpreter what type of variable it can expect *x* to be. The Assignment instruction assigns the value 500 (dollars) to variable *x*. This is just a starting value; the instructions in the Calculations section will probably alter the value of *x* during the course of the module. Finally, the Output instruction prints the value of *x* to the screen, with a dollar sign just to the left of it.

BASIC

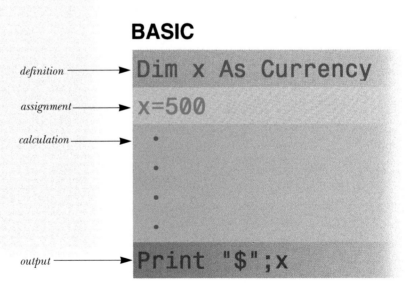

definition

assignment

calculation

output

```
Dim x As Currency
x=500
  .

  .

  .
Print "$";x
```

The Syntax of Modern Programming

All spoken or written languages can be broken down into structured parts; we refer to these parts as words, sentences, and paragraphs. Programming languages can also be broken down into structured parts; however, these parts have different names in most languages. In this chapter, we will refer to these parts as the instruction, keyword, and clause.

HERE'S AN UNUSUAL STATEMENT:
x = x + 1

How can the value of a variable be equal to the value of that same variable *plus one?* In algebra, this equation could not be true, because an equal sign in algebra is stating a fact—that x *does equal* 500. But, in a programming language, an equal sign is an instruction—set x *equal to* 500. Thus, x = x + 1 is valid in programming, because it is an instruction, but it is not valid in algebra, because it isn't a true fact. To add 1 to the value of whatever the current value of x is, in BASIC you can say x = x + 1. The variable to the left of the equal sign represents where to put the value, whereas the variable to the right of the equal sign represents what to put there. The instruction therefore reads, "Add 1 to whatever x contains now, and put it back into x."

The "sentence" of high-level programming is the *instruction.* One complete action—such as changing a variable's value or testing for a certain value—is an instruction. Within each instruction are *keywords* the compiler or interpreter instantly recognizes as part of the language's vocabulary. A keyword cannot be used for any purpose (in that language) other than its designated function.

Take the instruction For x = 1 To names. Here, the words For and To are keywords. The compiler recognizes these terms immediately, so the programmer cannot use them for any other purpose—such as variables. The term names in this instruction is *not* a keyword, so the programmer is free to use it as a variable.

DOES IT MATTER WHAT WE CALL THINGS?

It can be argued that the originators of different programming languages each subscribe to their own schools of thought. As a result, what one language calls an "instruction" another might call a "command," another a "directive," and another a "statement."

It is surprising that the components of high-level programming languages are far more alike in *concept* than they are in *name*. Despite the differences in names and physical structures, all high-level languages accomplish quite similar tasks through processes that are—behind the scenes—quite similar. In the next few pages, we focus on the underlying concepts of programming, sidestepping as many of these differences as possible.

Note: Every language has a list (some longer than others) of keywords that are reserved for specific purposes. The words Begin, End, For, Do, Repeat, Loop, Until, If, and Then are common keywords in most languages. Don't worry if you don't "recognize" keywords; they are different for every language and compiler. Programmers usually know only a small group of these keywords from memory, and must refer to manuals or books for a complete list of the keywords. The compiler, on the other hand, recognizes these keywords immediately.

Just as adjacent sentences are grouped into paragraphs, adjacent instructions are often grouped into a *clause*. Not all adjacent instructions form clauses, however. Clauses are groups of instructions that are executed contingent on some condition being True (or False). There is usually one instruction at the beginning of the clause (as you'll see later in this chapter) that can tell the computer to skip over the entire group of instructions. This initial instruction might test to see whether some variable has a particular value—if a variable is "over the limit." In Pascal, a clause consists of all the instructions between the keywords begin and end; in C and C++, a clause is identified with curly braces ({ and }).

THE LOOP CLAUSE

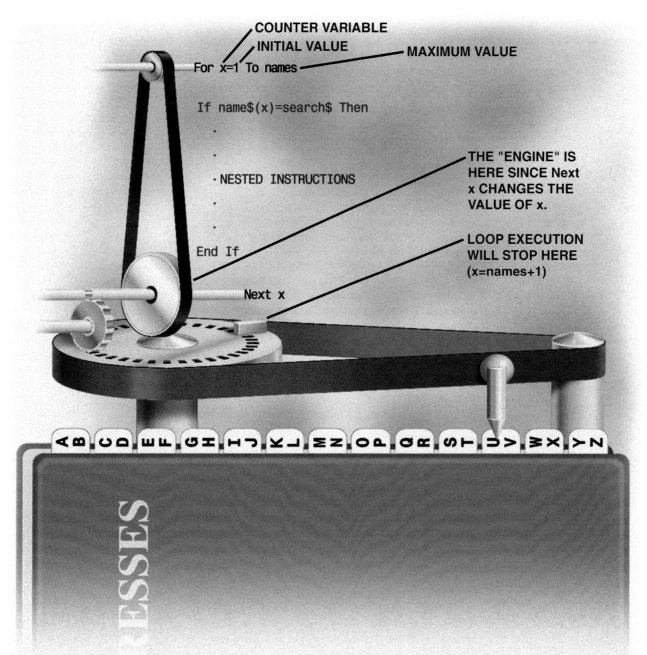

COUNTER VARIABLE
INITIAL VALUE
MAXIMUM VALUE

For x=1 To names

If name$(x)=search$ Then

· NESTED INSTRUCTIONS

End If

Next x

THE "ENGINE" IS HERE SINCE Next x CHANGES THE VALUE OF x.

LOOP EXECUTION WILL STOP HERE (x=names+1)

I n high-level programming languages, a loop clause is a way to take a group of adjacent instructions and say, "Everything from *this* line to *that* line will be repeated." If you need something done six times, you can have a loop clause count from one to six, and execute those instructions each time it counts.

You might be wondering why a programmer would need to repeat a clause—if something was done once, why does it need

to be done *again*? The main reason for a loop clause is to evaluate slightly varied conditions. Each time the instructions in the loop are executed, something changes.

In a For loop (shown here), the change is represented within the variable x. Each time the instructions in the loop are executed, 1 is added to the value of x. The *nested* instructions within the loop are re-executed each time x increases, because the results will be slightly different. This example uses a For

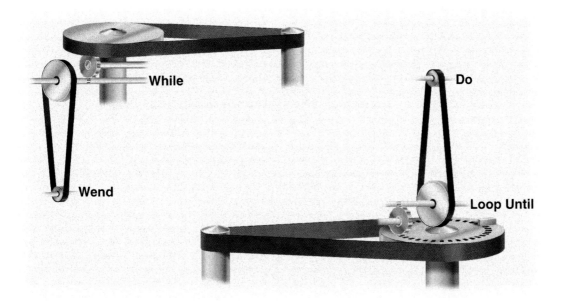

loop to locate a name in an address book. Variable x represents the entry (or person) in the address book being evaluated at the time: entry #1, entry #2, entry #3, and so on. The variable names represents the number of listings in the address book. The *programmer* doesn't know precisely how many listings there are—this number increases every time a name is added—but the *application* knows how many names are in the book, and that's what's important. When x is equivalent to the number of names in the book, the loop clause stops executing the nested instructions.

Now look closely at the For loop. The "engine" of the loop clause is at the bottom of the loop. The value of 1 is added to x when the program reaches Next x. The evaluation process (whether x = names) takes place here, not at the For instruction; that's why the engine is next to Next. Other forms of loop clauses have their "engines" in different places; for instance, BASIC's While-Wend loop has its engine at the beginning of the loop, whereas BASIC's Do-Loop Until loop has its engine at the end. Both loop clauses execute instructions *while* a certain mathematical condition is true; the difference between the two loops is that While-Wend tests for this condition at the beginning, before the loop is executed once, and Do-Loop-Until tests for this condition *after* the loop is executed once (or in programming terminology, after one *iteration* of the loop).

The For keyword is the same in Pascal and C++ as it was in the BASIC examples.

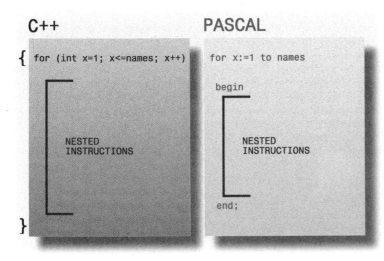

HOW CONDITIONAL CLAUSES WORK

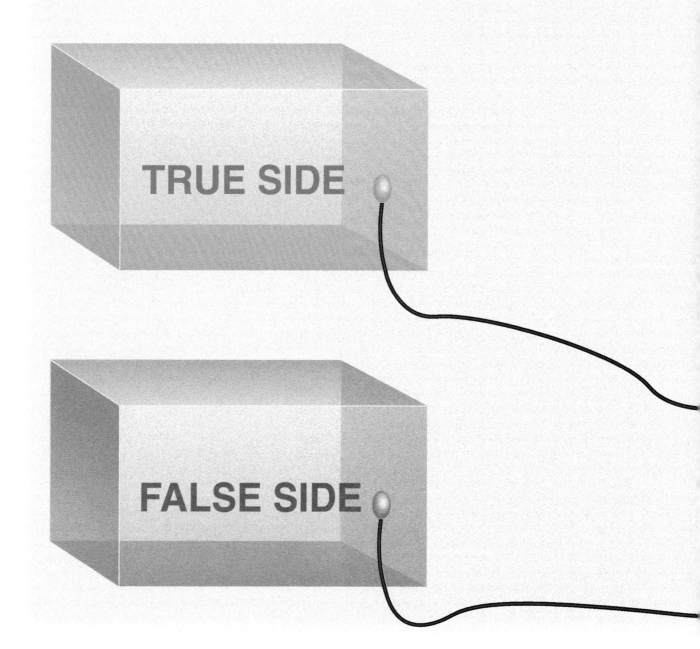

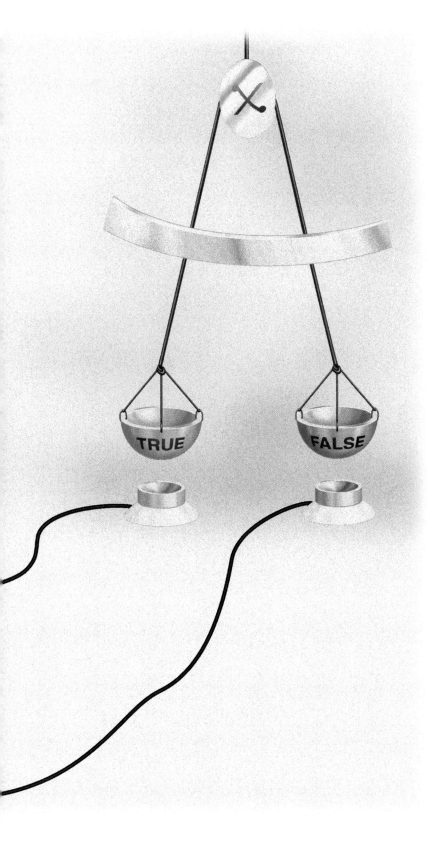

The most-used keyword in all high-level programming—BASIC, Pascal, C++, and even COBOL—is the If instruction. If makes it possible for a program to respond to certain conditions, rather than blindly execute instruction #1, instruction #2, and so on. A conditional clause in modern BASIC is bound by an If instruction at the beginning and an End If at the end. The clause shown here is constructed more like a double-decker hamburger. In the middle of this clause is an Else instruction, which effectively divides it into two halves. You can think of the upper half as the "True side" and the lower half as the "False side." Notice that the scales are next to the If instruction at the top; this is where the "engine" of the clause resides, and where the evaluation takes place.

The If conditional clause tests to see whether a certain condition is True. This condition is presented as a mathematical *expression*. This example continues the address book model from the previous page. This example tests the contents of a variable to see whether a particularly numbered name is equivalent to the name for which you are searching. The expression, in this case, is name$(x) = search$. Here the BASIC variables name$ and search$ contain text rather than numerical values; the dollar sign $ helps to distinguish this fact.

If the conditional test is True, the instructions nested within the True side of the clause are executed. If the condition proves false, the instructions in the False side are executed. Not all conditional clauses have False, or "Else," sides; however, they all have True sides.

The syntaxes for the If instruction in C++ and Pascal are remarkably similar to that of BASIC.

BRANCHING AND OTHER DIVERSIONS

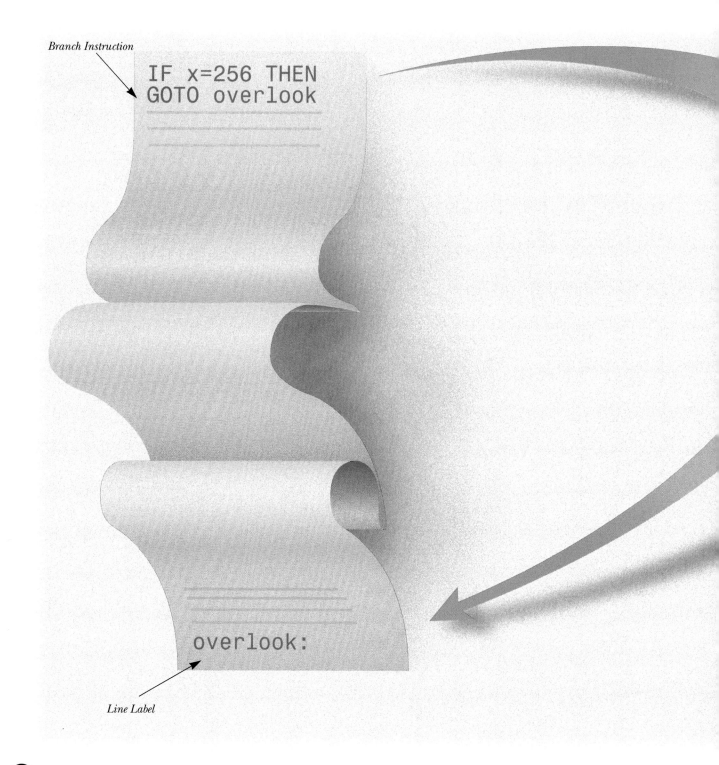

Branch Instruction

```
IF x=256 THEN
GOTO overlook
```

```
overlook:
```

Line Label

The *branch* instruction is a type of pointer that tells the computer where to go next. The simplest type of general branch instruction (in low- or high-level languages) is the type that basically states, "Don't execute the following instructions. Execute *these* instead." Because the branch diverts the program from running particular lines, branches are seldom used alone; instead they are often used in conjunction with conditions—most often the If instruction you saw in the preceding pages. Thus, *if* some condition is true, *then* avoid the following instructions.

In BASIC, the simplest branch instruction is called GoTo, as in "*go to* this other instruction." The instruction it branches to is preceded by a *label*; so the instruction If x = 256 Then GoTo overlook would take the computer to the section in the code labeled overlook, but *only* when variable x equals 256.

Today, many programmers frown on the use of simple branches. Source code based on the frequent use of simple branches has often been shunned as "spaghetti code"; it makes reading the source code difficult.

Instead of writing code with much branching, it is often recommended that you write *modular programs*, or *structured programs*, in which the program moves from one module to another. Structured programs move in a more ordered, adjacent pattern, and are much easier to follow than a program with many branching statements. In the next few pages, you see how subscribers to structured programming would rather arrange their branches, and why.

A group of BASIC-language instructions, called a *subroutine*, can be called by name from any area of the program using the GOSUB command. Although this method is now archaic, subroutines are still in use in many versions and dialects of BASIC today. Early BASIC programs required that each line of code have its own *line number*, so programmers could use GOSUB branch instructions to redirect execution to any particular line just by citing its number. The RETURN instruction was used at the end of the subroutine to close it and send execution back to the instruction following the GOSUB that called it, whichever and wherever that was.

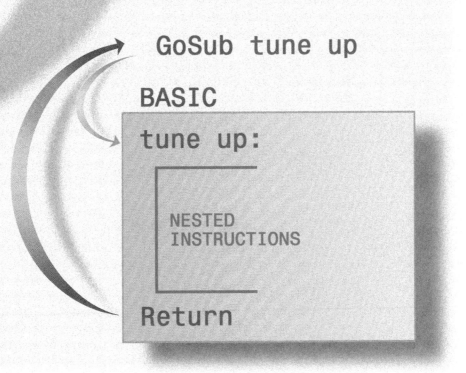

```
GoSub tune up

BASIC

tune up:


    NESTED
    INSTRUCTIONS



Return
```

MODULAR PROCEDURES AND PARAMETER PASSING

This text has touched on the subject of program modules several times; now it's time to see what it looks like to break source code into modules. This example comes from C++. In this language and its predecessor, C, all instructions must be written inside modules. Each module is presumed to have its own output value, which is signified here on the opening line—the *header* (note the printer cable inputting information). The term int (short for *integer*, or whole number) tells the compiler what type of number the compiler should expect for the module's output value. In this case, the compiler is looking for a whole number; it knows in advance there won't be any digits after the decimal point.

On the opening line, inside the parentheses, is a list of variables that will act as carriers of input values from the module that calls this module. In C and C++, a module is its own little world. It shares only as much "knowledge" of the outside world—of what values pertain to the modules outside of it—as the programmer dictates. The most important values from the outside world are listed in the *header* line—the opening line of a module.

Following the opening line is *definition section* in which a list of variables that pertain only to this module are defined. The compiler sees these definition lines and calls these variables into existence, although for now with null values. These variables are assigned values and manipulated throughout the *main calculations section* of the program. This section is where the actual actions and decisions take place.

The *output* value of a C++ module is set by means of the return instruction. (Notice the change box on the return line.) This is the value that this module will return to the module that called it. So a module takes a set of values (*parameters*), modifies them, and returns their product to the module that called this module.

Header

Definitions

Main calculations

Output

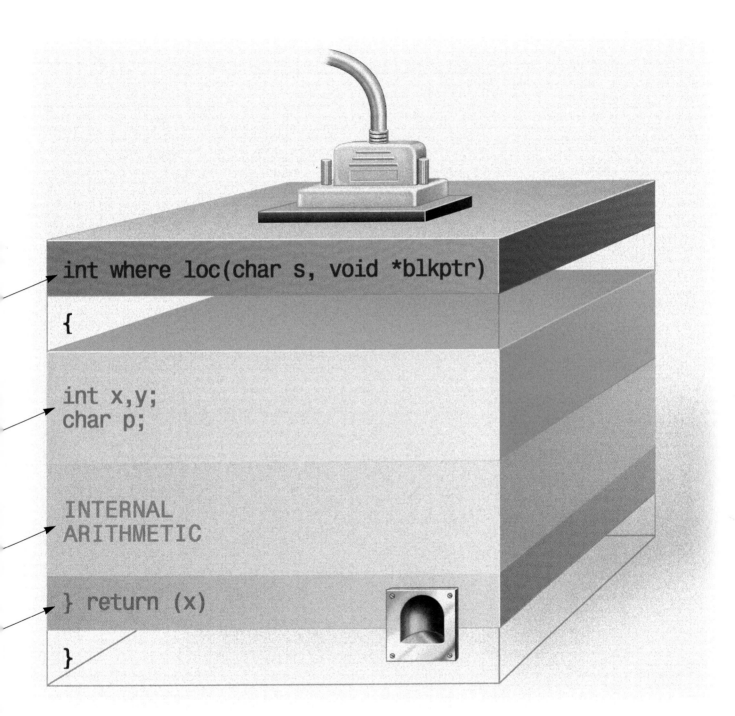

```
int where loc(char s, void *blkptr)

{

int x,y;
char p;

INTERNAL
ARITHMETIC

} return (x)

}
```

CHAPTER 4

MAKING NUMBERS PERFORM WORK

If you've ever looked at the main drawing screen of a computer-aided design (CAD) application such as AutoCAD, you've probably seen a skeletal representation of some real-world object—a building, a city, or the inside of a wristwatch—with lots of lines and measurement numbers all over it. When an architect designs a new object in his mind, he sees these numbers and measurements as *relationships* between one point and the next. He uses his own internal geometry to give him a mental preview of the sizes and proportions of things with respect to one another.

A computer programmer works in a similar manner. Everything a programmer builds must somehow be represented numerically. In addition to showing values and quantities, numbers can also act as symbols denoting the state of an item—such as *on* or *off*.

Sometimes this third use of numbers isn't as simple as on and off, however. Take, for instance, the many terms that a hospital applies to the status of a patient: good, stable, critical, and so on. There is an exact number of these status terms—about a dozen and no more. A computer is capable of storing these words in memory as *strings* of characters—"GOOD", "STABLE", and so on—but a medical application running on a computer has no understanding of these words or strings on its own. Just because a computer stores words in memory does not mean it gives them meaning.

Instead, the programmer would probably assign each status its own number or code value. A computer can store a number much more easily than it can store a string of characters. Furthermore, if "EXCELLENT" is number 1, "SERIOUS" is number 11, and "CRITICAL" is number 12, the *scale* that the programmer has created gives these symbols meanings that are relative to one another. A computer cannot naturally establish such relationships between words because it doesn't know *real* language.

WHAT OPERATORS DO

A t right is a BASIC language instruction that assigns a value to a variable. In this instance, the value is the result of a mathematical expression (the algebraic formula for the circumference of a circle). Some high-level languages automatically interpret pi as 3.1415927; for others, the programmer may have to assign that value to a variable pi in advance.

The equation multiplies 2 by pi and then by the value of r. In BASIC, Pascal, C++, and most other high-level languages, the asterisk * is used in place of the *x* to denote multiplication, because the computer could easily mistake *x* for a variable. The results of this equation are assigned to the variable c.

It's important to note here that a computer does not have an intrinsic understanding of algebraic formulas—even something as simple as finding the circumference of a circle. If the first instruction of a program stated c = 2 (pi) r, the result would always be the same—variable c would equal zero, because the computer was not told a value for r. The purpose of this instruction is to assign a value to c, but this will not work because the instruction can't be used to find a value for r, as in everyday algebra.

In "How Conditional Clauses Work" in the previous chapter, you saw how an If instruction determines which instructions to execute based on the results of a math test—a *mathematical expression*. Such an expression is written in the format at the bottom right: variable, operator, and expression.

48

Above, the math test is represented by a set of scales whose job it is to "weigh" the value of variable x in the left-side cup. For simplicity, we're comparing x to the unknown value of a variable y. You're probably familiar with the use of the math symbols > to denote "greater than" and < to denote "less than." To test whether the value of x is greater than that of y, the expression is written If x > y Then . . .. To test whether x is greater than *or equal to* y, you instead write x >= y. Such a test might be concerned with, for instance, whether the ratings for an automobile *meet or exceed* safety standards.

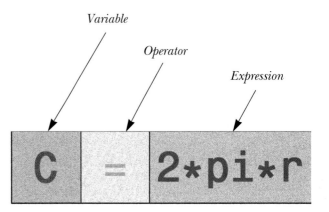

Variable

Operator

Expression

```
C  =  2*pi*r
```

Can You Really Define the World with Numbers?

As you begin to understand how computers count, you are beginning to understand the inspiration behind their invention. In 1854, British mathematician George Boole wrote a treatise theorizing that strictly binary logical processes (such as those just demonstrated) are the primary basis of all reasoning in the human mind. Boole believed that absolutely all thought could be broken into comparisons of True and False. It is for him that *Boolean logic* (one of the subjects of Chapter 5) is named.

Charles Babbage is credited with inventing the calculating device. There is considerable argument over whether Babbage's devices were really computers, because they were not electronic; but then again, neither was anything else in Babbage's day. The concept of an electronic computer was brought forth, in large part, by a Hungarian physicist named John von Neumann. In the late 1930s, von Neumann studied Boole's works thoroughly and, employing a natural skepticism for which the world will be forever thankful, bent Boole's logic so that it applied not to mental processes but to *physical* processes. He saw

that electrical devices perform the same function, mathematically speaking, as Boole's math.

John von Neumann was an acknowledged master of using mathematics to "prove" just about anything. In his 1932 book, von Neumann also managed to disprove the existence of every-thing—at least in the literal sense. One of his theories stated, in general, that because people apply different symbols to everyday things to help their minds reason with them, the universe is really comprised *only* of those symbols, and that they exist *only* in the mind and nowhere else. His proof was based on the same type of logic that led to the invention of the electronic computer and the stored symbolic program.

SPOTLIGHT ON ARRAY VARIABLES

When creating a program that must maintain a list of data, such as the number of students enrolled in each of a school's classes or the number of employees in each of a company's departments, it gets cumbersome to have a separate variable for each class or department—Department_1$,

`Department_2$`, `Department_3$`, and so on. Also, it is impossible to use `For` loops to sort through variables of different names, because a loop always repeats the same statement.

Now look at the following two instructions:

```
Class(1) = 18
Class(2) = 21
```

This might look a little confusing. It seems that both `18` and `21` are assigned to the same variable—`Class`. But actually, `Class` is an *array variable*. The numbers in parentheses following the variable name indicate that `Class` is an array variable (or array). You can think of an array as a chest of drawers, in which each drawer (or *cell*, as they are usually called) holds a separate variable of the same type. In this case, the array `Class` has two cells, each containing an integer variable. Drawer one, labeled `Class(1)` in BASIC, contains `18`, and drawer 2, `Class(2)`, contains `21`. The *tag number*—1 and 2—identifies which cell of the array is being looked at.

Arrays are useful in maintaining lists of data. If a programmer created an array to hold the class sizes for a school with 20 classes, he would need to remember only one variable name rather than 20 separate variables. Also, the program can search the list of names using a `For` loop, such as the following:

```
For x = 1 to 25
  If Class(x) = 21 Then
    Print x
  End If
Next x
```

This loop searches all 25 cells, one at a time, of the `Class` array, looking for classes with 21 students. The first statement creates the variable `x`, which is later used in the second statement to represent *each* of the tag numbers from `x` to `25`, incremented by the `Next x` statement. If the value of the current cell is equal to 21, the third statement prints the cell number. The `For` loop then starts all over again. Without an array, this search would have taken 20 or more instructions.

HOW PROGRAMS EXPRESS RELATIONSHIPS

Here are some further examples of the use of comparison operators in high-level languages, only this time they're applied to strings of characters (such as words). The $ symbol is placed beside a BASIC variable name to tell the interpreter that the variable represents a string rather than a value. This way, the compiler won't try to multiply 6 by "Roger".

To the left of the address book in this sketch are several BASIC instructions that involve expressions. The "on" light bulbs represent True statements and the "off" light bulbs represent False statements. The first expression, "Nolan is less than Palmer," surprisingly turns out to be True. This is because N falls earlier in the alphabet than P.

For this example, the string array c$ holds the last names of people listed in the address book. (In BASIC, the $ character indicates that c contains a string.) The second and third instructions assign the names Palmer and Nolan to the first and second cells of string array c$, respectively. The fourth instruction merely proves that 2 is not less than 1, even though Nolan (in cell 2) is less than Palmer (in cell 1).

In the fifth statement, when the first cell of c$ is compared to the second cell, Nolan again proves to be "less than" Palmer. Here, unlike the first instruction, the variable names are used in place of the actual names. This instruction is more versatile than the first statement, because it can be used even if names other than Nolan and Palmer are later assigned to cells c$(1) and c$(2).

```
"Nolan" < "Palmer"

c$(1) = "Palmer"

c$(2) = "Palmer"

2 < 1

c$(2) < c$(1)

Len (c$(1)) > Len (c$(2))

x = 2

c$(x) = "Nolan"

max = 8

Len (c$(2)) > max
```

The next instruction shows a BASIC language *function* called Len() that tests for the number of letters contained within a string variable. Palmer is longer than Nolan, so the test for whether the length of c$(1) is greater than c$(2) also proves True.

The next instruction assigns 2 to the variable x. In the following statement, the programmer checks to see if c$(x)—cell 2, in this case—is Nolan.

Finally, the last two instructions show that a test resulting in False may also be quite helpful. max = 8 states that eight is the maximum number of characters for any name in your database. The final instruction verifies that Nolan is not longer than eight characters.

BINARY VALUES AS FLAGS

In the last section, "How Programs Express Relationships," you saw several math expressions whose results were shown to be "True" or "False." The computer stores the values True and False as binary digits (bits), with False equalling 0 and True equalling 1. Using this system, the results of a True/False math expression (x = 5) can be assigned to a variable.

Earlier, we mentioned how number values may be assigned to variables as a way of showing some state or condition. Such variables are termed *flags*, which is a reference to the flagmen on ships and airport runways that signal the actions of the ship or aircraft. In this sketch, a set of five flags represents the status of a file being managed by an application. A file that has been saved, for example, may be symbolized by a 1 (the "backed up" flag). Once the user makes an entry into a new and open document, however, the application may respond internally by assigning 3 (altered) to the file status variable without the user knowing this has happened. In fact, hundreds of such status variables are maintained all the time without the user knowing.

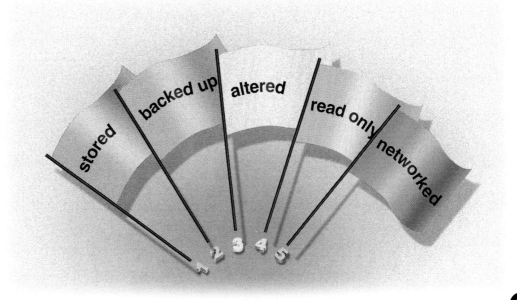

THE QUANTIZED WORLD
OF AN APPLICATION

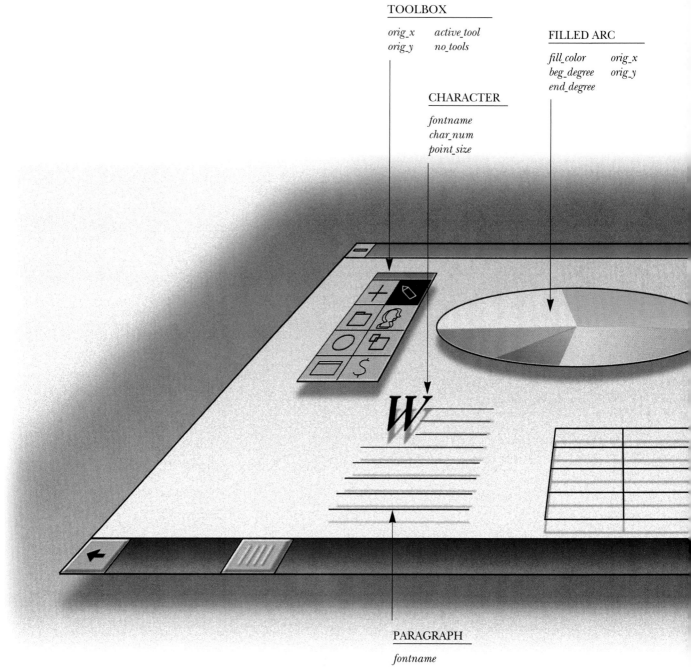

TOOLBOX

orig_x   *active_tool*
orig_y   *no_tools*

CHARACTER

fontname
char_num
point_size

FILLED ARC

fill_color   *orig_x*
beg_degree   *orig_y*
end_degree

PARAGRAPH

fontname
point_size
contents_file

Every component of a computer application is, in some way, numbered. It's given some variable representative of some quantity or symbol. Here we've laid out an application on the table to show you just a few of the items in which status variables would apply, along with the names that might be applied to those variables.

Almost every graphical object in an application has data associated with it denoting its relative location on the screen—geometrically speaking, its *coordinates*. The position of the toolbox, and the arc center of each pie slice in the chart, may be determined by using such coordinates. Imported items, such as the bitmapped photograph and the text file, have status variables as well.

The source code of an application does two things with status variables. It either assigns flag values to them, or it tests those values by using a conditional clause. Besides the underlying math and data management, an application maintains its own internal world of symbols. A programmer chooses symbols, symbol names, and flag values arbitrarily— it's all a matter of good design practices rather than rules set in stone.

DRAW TOOL

pen_color
active
draw_width
xpos
ypos

BITMAP

filename
contrast
resolution

SCROLL BOX

ypos
step_value

TABLE CELL

row
column
format
contents

USING ALGEBRA TO DESIGN RULES

If you've ever played a game of Reversi on a computer, you've probably been beaten at least once or twice, and wondered how or why. Perhaps you imagined just what formula a Reversi game uses to pick the right (or even the wrong) moves and beat a human player. If such a formula exists within a computer program, why doesn't anyone tell us humans what it is?

You might be surprised to learn that there is no such formula. Reversi (or chess or checkers) programs use no formal strategies. Instead, they employ repetitious bodies of code called *algorithms* (remember the Recipe section from Chapter 1?) to analyze every possible move on the board at any one time.

Below is a view of the Reversi board in a way you generally don't see it. Here, the green squares are considered the "best" squares by Reversi masters, and the red squares the "worst." Using symbolic variables, it's possible to tell a Reversi program which squares are the best on a relative scale, perhaps with a positive number denoting benefit and a negative number denoting danger.

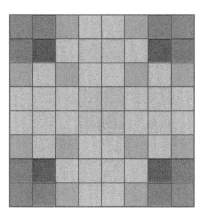

No program—no person, for that matter— can win at Reversi just on that knowledge. From there, the program must analyze every possible move, along with every possible human player response to those moves, every possible computer player response to those responses, and so on until the program runs out of either memory or time.

Take the larger Reversi board as an example. It's white's move, and among the squares under consideration are the two transparent tokens. One of these moves is legal, and the other illegal. The objective of Reversi is to capture pieces and turn them over to your color, by surrounding a string of your opponent's pieces on two sides with pieces of your own. In the computer's memory, white squares may be symbolized with a positive 1 value for each square, black squares with a negative 1, and empty squares with 0. To determine whether a move is legal, the Reversi algorithm must search for adjacent enemy squares. The way the internal math is set up here, all it needs

to do is look for surrounding squares whose values are *negative* with regard to its own. Once the algorithm finds a negative value, it follows that string of squares until it finds a positive value again (but not a zero value). Once that happens, the move is proclaimed legal. Legality and illegality can be represented in the program by a flag variable as well.

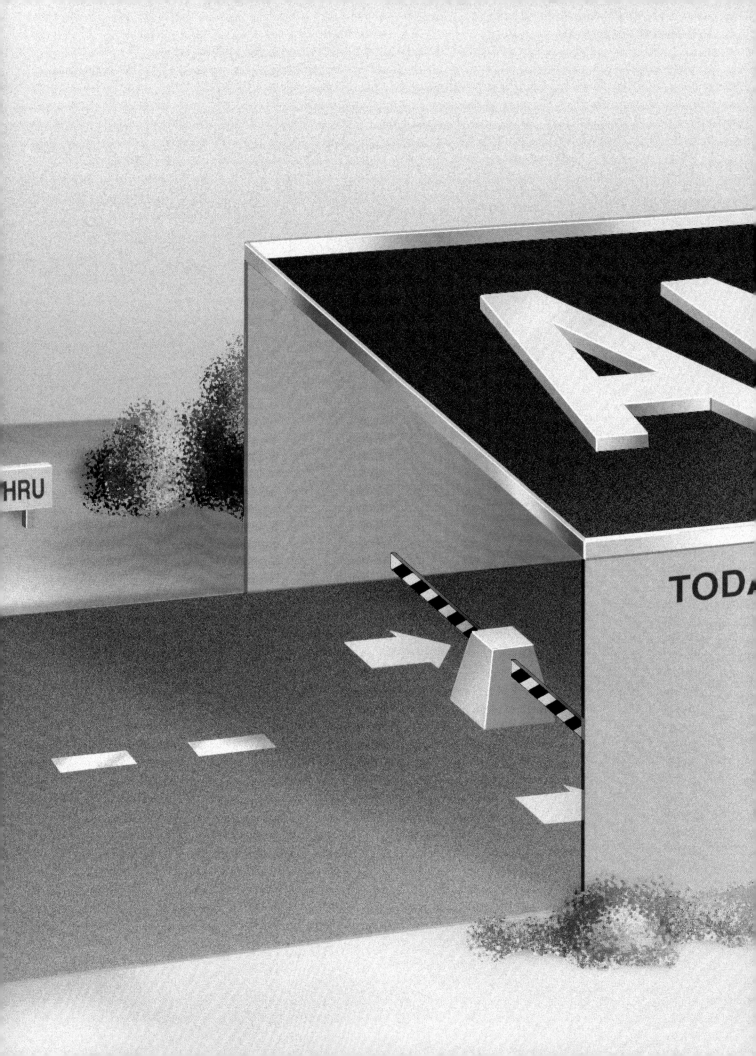

CHAPTER 5

THE COMPUTER'S ENGINE

The term *algorithm* is Arabic and means "repetitive math." A computer algorithm is a set of instructions repeated many times until a desired answer is found. Often, an algorithm cannot know in advance how many times it has to repeat itself before its job is complete; however, it does know when the job is complete.

An algorithm in modern computing performs repetitious, often tedious, processes. Sorting a list, picking the top 10 elements from multiple lists, searching a list for a desired name, and finding the best move in a game of Reversi are processes best handled by algorithms.

Algorithms are the lifeblood of advanced computing. What a computer really does best is process and find new ways to examine data that otherwise appears meaningless to human beings. For example, sorting a list of 10 million names is no more difficult for a computer than sorting a list of 10, as long as the computer has access to enough memory. The computer uses the same process each time—and it doesn't sweat or complain about it along the way. The reason for this efficiency is the inherent simplicity—even beauty—of algorithms. To understand them is to comprehend the basic processes of the computer itself.

HOW A COMPUTER COUNTS

$$01001101_2$$

128 64 32 16 8 4 2

1   1   1

64 + 8 + 4 +

Our common system of counting is called *decimal* because *deci-* is a Greek prefix meaning *10*. Fractional values that we use every day are sometimes called *decimal numbers*, perhaps because such numbers force you to use the *decimal point* to separate the whole number side from the fractional side. In our everyday world, all numbers we use to count with are decimal numbers. Our decimal numbering system is called *base 10*.

The number *77* is a decimal number because you trust it to be written in base 10. At least you assume it's a decimal number,

because there's nothing here to tell you otherwise. In base 16 (*hexadecimal*) notation, "77" does not mean "seventy-seven," but instead means "one hundred nineteen." Computers use hexadecimal numbers all the time, but not nearly as often as they use the simplest number system ever devised—the *binary* system.

Human beings find it easy to count in decimal numbers—probably because we have 10 fingers on which to count. All of our math is originally based on counting on our fingers. Computers don't have fingers to count on. The closest thing they have are the two electrical states inside the computer: on and as 01001101, as demonstrated here. You can see the places for each binary digit written above the "bit cage" shown at the left of this page. We've placed a 1 "bit-ball" inside each box whose place is part of the sum of 77; the 1 shows that this bit is positive, or turned "on." The ones place, the fours place, the eights place, and the sixty-fours place are all occupied by bit-balls.

At right is a list of 16 values, 0 through 15. The first column shows the numbers in the familiar decimal, base 10 system. The second column shows them in the hexadecimal, base 16 language used by many programming languages (2 x 2 x 2 x 2). Finally, the graph shows the same numbers written as four-bit binary numbers. Notice that only one hexadecimal digit is required for values through 15, but because we run out of numbers after 9, we resort to using A, B, C, D, E, and F to represent the remaining six numbers.

1 = 77₁₀

off. We usually refer to "on" as 1 and "off" as 0, so we can relate it back to numbers we can understand. Thus, a computer counts only with the numbers 0 to 1, rather than 0 to 9, like we do. Binary math is natural for a computer. Computers find it difficult to do math in our decimal number system, because 10 can't easily be expressed as a power of 2; the closest it comes is 2 x 5— and the five can't be broken down any further.

The number 5 written in base 2 (binary) format appears as 101. In other words, there's a 1 in the fours place and a 1 in the ones place. The value 77 is written in binary

D	H	B			
0	0	0	0	0	0
1	1	0	0	0	1
2	2	0	0	1	0
3	3	0	0	1	1
4	4	0	1	0	0
5	5	0	1	0	1
6	6	0	1	1	0
7	7	0	1	1	1
8	8	1	0	0	0
9	9	1	0	0	1
10	A	1	0	1	0
11	B	1	0	1	1
12	C	1	1	0	0
13	D	1	1	0	1
14	E	1	1	1	0
15	F	1	1	1	1

ALL A COMPUTER DOES
IS COMPARE

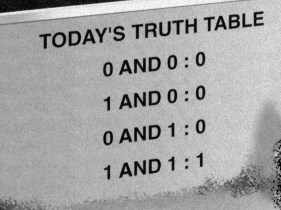

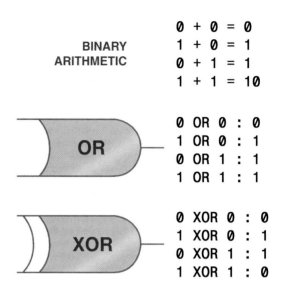

BINARY ARITHMETIC	0 + 0 = 0
	1 + 0 = 1
	0 + 1 = 1
	1 + 1 = 10

OR	0 OR 0 : 0
	1 OR 0 : 1
	0 OR 1 : 1
	1 OR 1 : 1

XOR	0 XOR 0 : 0
	1 XOR 0 : 1
	0 XOR 1 : 1
	1 XOR 1 : 0

High-level programming languages shield the programmer from having to deal directly with the circuitry of the computer's internal processors. Nonetheless, *Boolean logic*—which is taking place here—is concerned entirely with comparing two signals and outputting one. If you could look inside a processor, you'd discover that this is really all a computer does.

So why does it look to everyone else as if a computer is processing text and saving databases? Part of the answer has to do with what these comparisons actually *do*. On the right side of the sketch is a table of the only four combinations of digits you'll need to add together in binary arithmetic. Below that are two other types of Boolean electronic gates, called OR and XOR (or *exclusive-OR*). An exclusive-OR results in a 1 (True) if one incoming signal is *not* like the other—the opposite of an AND. Notice something interesting about these tables: The XOR truth table renders much the same results as the binary arithmetic table; the only difference is that in binary 1 + 1, you carry the left digit to the left to make 10 (that's really two, not 10). The XOR process therefore can be made to simulate addition. Other combinations of binary gates can simulate other ordinary math processes; by doing so, these simulations make up the heart of all computer science. All basic math is simulated by means of Boolean logic gates.

T he key electronic components of a computer's internal central processing unit (CPU) are referred to as a *logic gate*. The AND gate is represented in this sketch by a drive-through car wash—except that there are two entrances and one exit. Two cars (or signals) enter and one car (or signal) comes out. Whether the outgoing signal is a 0 or 1 depends entirely on the identity of the incoming signals. The table that determines the value of the outgoing signal is called the *truth table*—partly because you can rely on this table to always be correct.

In the AND gate shown here, the outgoing signal will be 1 (True) if the two incoming signals are identical—one AND the other, in other words. If they're not identical, the signal will be 0 (False).

Algo-What???

The purpose of algorithms may not be clear to you even yet, but don't worry; this isn't an easy topic to follow. Perhaps the best way to understand algorithms is to take computers out of the picture altogether for a moment.

Imagine that you're alphabetizing the contents of your file drawer. What's the most efficient method you can use to organize your files? Perhaps when you first start sorting the files, you don't have a formal method; but the more you sort the files, the more you find your mind developing a method for putting the files in order.

One method developed by librarians is to divide the file drawer contents into two sections—"finished" and "unfinished." You take the first file from the unfinished section and place it in the finished section in alphabetical order. As the finished section grows, the unfinished section shrinks. When you start sorting like this day after day, eventually you stop actually *thinking* about your work, and just let the lower-level processes of your mind take over while you daydream.

Because the underlying process of file sorting is so simple—the same few steps repeated hundreds of times—you can execute this process yourself without really "thinking" about it. Surprisingly enough, so can the computer. An algorithm is a simple, repetitive process—like your directions for "How to Sort Your File Drawer," if you were to write

them down. The best and most elegant algorithms are often the simplest and smallest ones.

ALGORITHMS AND YOUR CD PLAYER

One of the amazing things about a compact disc player is that it continues to produce clear and perfect songs even when the disc is damaged. Perhaps even more amazing, however, is that the sounds emerging from the damaged parts of a CD are often produced not by the disc, but by the computer inside the CD player, after having estimated what the damaged sound should be.

Every CD player maintains in its memory a continually changing list of sound probabilities, based on the sounds it has "heard" thus far. First, a CD player reads the same sector of the disc multiple times and checks for differences each time. Next, the CD player uses its own internal algorithms to predict when a sound falls outside the current range of sound possibilities. This gives the CD player a certain degree of error prediction.

When the CD player thinks it has found an error, it checks to see which sounds have most often followed the sound just before the error occurred, and gives that sound a try. Because defects in CDs are so minimal in size and scope, even if the CD player guesses wrong, the length of the incorrect sound will probably be so short that it will go unheard.

HOW AN ALGORITHM SORTS DATA

The illustration on this page represents a program, with the QuickSort algorithm highlighted. Just as breaking down a program into smaller parts makes programming easier, breaking down the large list takes much of the complexity out of the sorting task.

Earlier, we mentioned how one sorting algorithm divides the records to be sorted into two sections, "finished" and "unfinished." QuickSort is different in that it uses a "two-handed" approach. Imagine a row of books on a shelf in front of you. In your mind, place your hands on the first and last books in the row. Look at the first book (in your left hand) and the last book (in your right hand). Searching from the last book forward through the shelf, look for the first book that belongs *before* the first book on the shelf. When you find it, swap the two books. Next, look at the last book; beginning with the first book on the shelf, look for the first book, from left to right, that belongs *after* the last book, and swap them.

Eventually, as this goes on, the positions of your hands will collide with one another. When this happens, your shelf won't be sorted yet, but it'll be closer to sorted than it was. The books to the left of your left hand *will belong to the left*, and those to the right of your right hand will belong there. You now have two "subsections" that you can sort individually.

This process might sound a bit tedious and, on the whole, not at all fun. For the QuickSort algorithm, however, it's no problem. For large lists, it takes QuickSort fewer swaps (what programmers call *iterations*) to achieve perfect order than for any other algorithm yet discovered. QuickSort is therefore more efficient, because it divides large lists into smaller, more manageable lists.

There are several efficient ways to sort numbers or names in a list, but none so far have proven more efficient for all-around tasks than what is called the QuickSort algorithm, an old-faithful used by programmers at all levels. There are two secrets to this time-tested routine: First, it takes one big list and effectively separates it into smaller lists that are easier to manage. Second, it uses a back-and-forth method for swapping the places of two elements in the list with one another.

The QuickSort array would sort a large list of numbers (such as the file shown on the left) as several smaller lists (the separate rows).

FINDING ONE IN A BILLION

Olin?

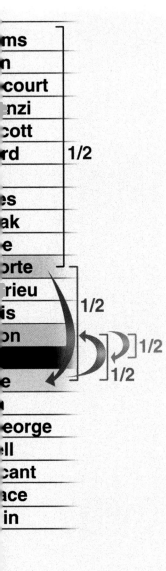

You've seen a computer produce your name and address from a set of records in a database faster than you can start a stopwatch. Perhaps you've wondered whether the list was alphabetized; if so, wouldn't it take longer for the computer to pull up a record for a person whose name begins with Z than it does for a person with a name beginning with A? It doesn't appear to take any longer, but is this just an optical illusion, because the computer is so fast anyway?

If a computer really were to search for a record starting at the top of the file and working back one-by-one, no matter how fast the computer, you'd notice the wait for Mr. Zoeller's record to come up. The reason computers work so fast in the first place is due in large part to algorithms in the programming. All database programs implement search algorithms that use math to help the computer find a particular record.

This illustration shows the most common search algorithm employed today, the binary search, being used to sort through our address book. The algorithm pulls up a record in the exact *middle* of the data file. Some database programs call this record the "cursor" location. The algorithm then tests to see whether the cursor's contents (in this case, the last name) match the name being searched for; chances are, it probably *will not* match. So using the greater-than and less-than (> and <) comparison operators, the algorithm tests to see whether the searched-for name lies before or after the current record. After the algorithm has made that determination, the search pattern *jumps* exactly half the distance between one end of the file and the current location. This jump is in the direction determined by the greater-than/less-than comparison.

Next, the algorithm tests the record currently under the cursor; again, if this algorithm isn't the one being searched for, the algorithm jumps again. This time, the jump distance is exactly half that of the previous jump, in the direction determined by the greater-than/less-than comparison. After playing "higher" or "lower" with the computer enough times, eventually the cursor lands on the right record.

How soon is "eventually?" For data files containing 10,000 or more records, the algorithm will find the right record after no more than 14 attempts (iterations). Believe it or not, for our address book with 22 names, this illustration correctly shows that it will take only four iterations.

ADDING AN INDEX TO THE DATABASE

NAME	INDEX ADDRESS
Morris	1217
Nelson	464
Olin	561
Petrie	12
Ryan	1341

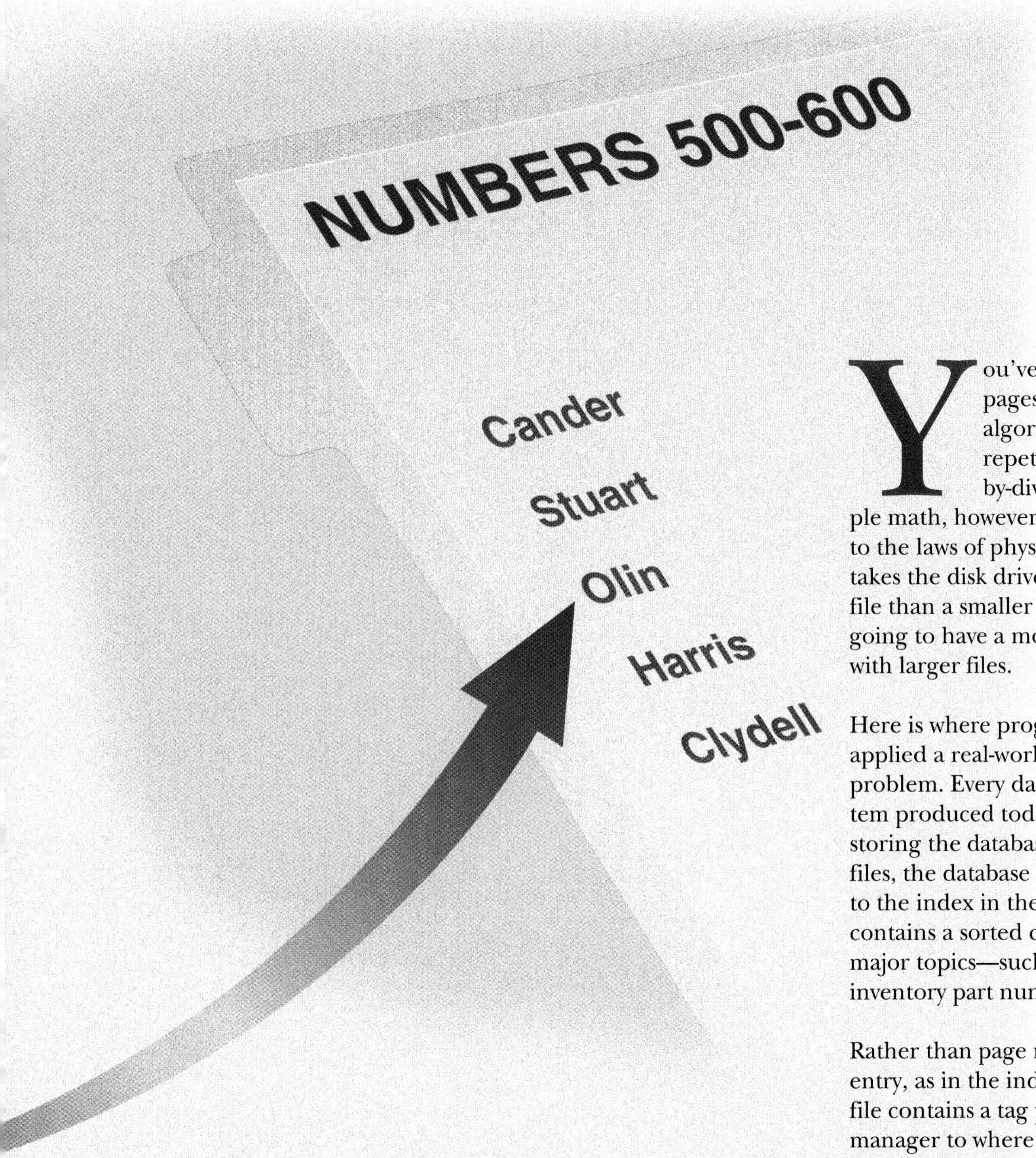

NUMBERS 500-600

Cander

Stuart

Olin

Harris

Clydell

You've seen in the past few pages how programmers write algorithms that attack large, repetitive tasks in a conquer-by-dividing fashion. Even simple math, however, must at times give way to the laws of physics. Simply because it takes the disk drive longer to read a larger file than a smaller one, any algorithm is going to have a more difficult time dealing with larger files.

Here is where programmers again have applied a real-world solution to a computer problem. Every database-management system produced today uses *indexing* when storing the database. In addition to its data files, the database has an index file, similar to the index in the back of a book, that contains a sorted copy of the key fields, or major topics—such as customer names or inventory part numbers.

Rather than page numbers next to each entry, as in the index of a book, the index file contains a tag pointing the database manager to where the *real* record is located in the main data file. Therefore, when a database search is performed, the database management system (DBMS) uses the index file to find the record. Because the index is a smaller file than the main file, the overall search becomes even faster.

In this illustration, the search algorithm looks for `Olin` in the index, on the left, and finds the index address of 561. The algorithm then turns to the relevant section of the database, shown on the right, and looks for the index address—in this case, `500-600`. Using indexing in the search algorithm tremendously increases the speed of the search.

**CUSTOMER
invoice**

RETAILER

CHAPTER 6

HOW DATA WORKS

The most overlooked aspect of developing an application is that the programmer must also design the application (format the data). If you've ever used more than one brand of word processor, database manager, or graphics design application, you know that formatting data is a headache!

What makes modern operating environments work so well (or rather, what is supposed to make them work so well) is the way their applications share data with one another. The problem is, part of what gives a software manufacturer the right to retain its brand name is its uniqueness. A word processor is generally free to use its own unique data format. A database management system (DBMS), however, must be capable of distributing records of people, places, accounts, and events to other systems on and off the network. To do this, it must import and export in a data format that isn't as specialized. One system must be capable of interpreting the data provided to it by all the other systems connected to it and communicating with it.

The language of an application is therefore not the programming language in which it was written, but the data format. Most database managers are written in dBASE format. Most major word processors can save a report in one of many general text formats, or a more specific, unique format. A digitized photograph can be stored in one of thousands of formats, depending on the number of colors contained in the photo, the amount of contrast, the level of compression, and so on. One of the most popular programs currently sold to typesetters is a picture format converter.

Distributed data is computer data that is stored in a file on a disk and given to someone else. The most common means of maintaining this distributed data is in table format—the main focus of this chapter.

THE CONSTITUTION OF DATA

FORM

Item No.　Qty.

Descrip.

Cost　Vend.　Source

Item No.　Qty.　Description

Corre

You're already familiar with the use of the term "table" to describe a set of data. At the front of this book is a table of contents. Many games of Solitaire call the card pile you combine in front of you "your table." Throughout history, a table has been a container of things. When books were bound with clay plates, they were called tables. Smaller bound sheets of wood became tablets.

Because data has been placed on tables throughout history, it seems fitting that we represent data as a table here. The wooden table in this sketch shows a set of data in a spreadsheet application (such as Microsoft Excel or Lotus 1-2-3). This abbreviated table contains an inventory list with six fields. Each field, represented by one column, is an important element of the inventory process—such as Item No. or Cost.

Each row in the inventory table is one record. A description of one item of inventory is a record—it's all the things that relate to one another. Keep in mind the term "relate," because you'll read it often in this chapter.

A person entering a record into a data table might use a form like the one shown here.

When a data table is attached to a letter of correspondence such as this document, the word processor is generally smart enough to correctly format the columns. Once this document is stored to disk, those spaces and tabs are saved as part of the document.

The original file containing the data table is far more conservative. Most data file formats contain a "header" that describes the length and data type of each field in a record. The file, therefore, doesn't need the spaces and tabs to keep it formatted; all it needs are "fenceposts" between fields, identifying the end of one field and the beginning of another. Whichever application is responsible for importing the data table into the document—the word processor or the database manager—must be smart enough to restyle the appearance of the field contents so that you can read them when they're printed.

THE RELATIONSHIPS IN A DATABASE

Large, multinational corporations use databases whose records are distributed across continents. Even though divisions may be continents apart, the corporate database may contain information that each division needs to use.

Any one person, whatever continent he happens to be on, won't be able to make much sense of this information unless he can see how the records pertain to one another. The user of a database manager should not have to play detective. The relationships between data—what was purchased, when, from whom, who made it, what was the purchase order number, and so on—should be obvious. For this reason, some programmers design their data tables—the physical records—to be large and to contain all of the possible information about an item.

CUSTOMER
invoice

RETAILER
restock order

WAREHOUS
purchase ord

Who Purchased It?
What Was Purchased?
What Was Its Cost?
When Was It Stocked?
When Was It Ordered?
Who Distributes It?
When Do We Reorder It?
What Is Its Catalog Number?
Who Manufactures It?
How Long Is Its Warranty?
When Will It Be Discontinued?

The reports regularly generated by different offices use only certain elements of the large table of information. The corporation's retail outlet, for example, might not need to know when the purchased item will be discontinued by the manufacturer. This is an important piece of information to somebody, so it's still a part of the physical record. Each division's regular reports, however, may contain only subdivisions, or logical records, of the main physical record.

MANUFACTURER
catalog

WHOLESALER
merchandise order

Standardization versus Specialization

The text you are reading now is data. The file my word processor produced while this chapter was being typed, however, was not composed solely of the letters and numbers you're reading on this page. Someplace in the document file, generally in the header, is a segment of even more data that explains to the word processor how this text is supposed to be formatted. This segment of data is often generically called formatting information.

The data within the header of a document file "teaches" the word processor how to format and regulate this particular document. These codes pertain to the specific word processor—how it manages margins, font sizes, leading between lines, and so on. Because no two word processors have the same list of features, no two document file formats are identical.

When you pick up a book, you automatically know how to use the lines and spaces to direct your eyes from word to word. A word processor knows less about how to read a new document file than you do. It is up to the header data to train the word processor, literally, about how to read it. At first, the word processor doesn't "see" the edges of the page, the spaces between words, or the placement of words on a line. It can "see" this only

after using the header to decipher the characters of data that follow the header.

So in a sense, when a programmer designs the format for document headers, he is creating a programming language. The contents of this language are instructional. Some header formats even contain conditional instructions, to be interpreted only under certain circumstances.

THE DIFFERENCE BETWEEN DATA AND INFORMATION

Some texts use the terms "data" and "information" interchangeably. Any professional programmer will tell you, however, that these two terms refer to entirely different concepts. Information is something that tells you, the human being, something you did not know before. Data is the storage medium for information housed temporarily within a computer, as it is being transported from person to person.

Data is like a container; but, it's no more the information than the can is the soup. Data is meaningless to the computer; only language instructions are meaningful. Many algorithms may be used to make data meaningless to people unless they have a program that uses a certain mathematical formula to decipher it— much like using a "secret decoder."

SPOTLIGHT ON WAYNE RATLIFF

More than 70 percent of the world's tabular micro-computer data is stored in the xBASE format. The sole designer of the first edition of this format was C. Wayne Ratliff, who at the time was an employee of Martin Marietta Corp., working under contract for the Jet Propulsion Laboratory (JPL) in Pasadena, California. Ratliff did not design the inspiration for the xBASE format, called MFILE, for wide public use—not even for use on Earth. MFILE was used by the Viking lander as it acquired soil samples on Mars.

In 1976, Ratliff decided to design another MFILE concept for use on Earth, especially for help in deciphering football statistics. In his spare time at home, Ratliff built a computer from a kit, and devised a programming language similar to one used at JPL. His mission: To devise a system for pre-dicting the results of next Sunday's NFL games. He called his language implementation Vulcan. He sold the marketing rights to the product to a small compa-ny called Discount Software, which later transferred them to Ashton-Tate Corp., where the product was renamed dBASE.

Perhaps even more important than the dBASE lan-guage itself, Ratliff introduced one other innovation to microcomputing: the attachment of the header to the data file itself. Previously, the format of the data-base or data table was specified by separate files or just in the memory of the database manager itself. The attached header allowed data files to be trans-portable with format, instructions, and data intact as one file—for the first time.

STRUCTURED QUERIES

When a computer system or network maintains a complete database, any request made of that database is treated as a query. The Structured Query Language (or SQL, pronounced "sequel") is a set of terms used by many database programming languages (including dBASE and Oracle) to easily retrieve one or more records of data based on certain mathematical criteria.

In this sketch, the meaning of the SQL instruction at left is easily interpretable even at first glance. The SQL programmer wants from the inventory table a list of all item numbers, item descriptions, and their costs, for all cases in which the cost is below $50.

The table at the right shows the three columns of data being queried; their telephone poles are each connected to the SQL SELECT statement at left. Specifically, the contents of the cost column (the column to be tested) are being examined.

SELECT item no. desc, cos

FROM inventory

WHERE cost < 50

BUILDING QUERIES INTO APPLICATIONS

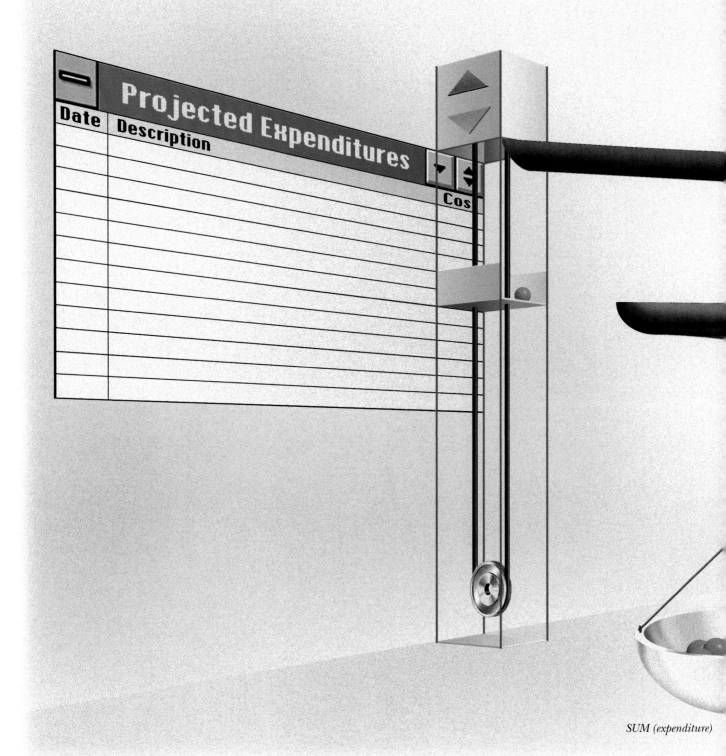

SUM (expenditure)

The backbone of most single-purpose or vertical-market applications programmed today is one or two simple database queries. One primary function of the Quicken accounting program, for example, is to accumulate the sum of one's projected expenditures, and to compare this sum against the projected budget. This procedure, from the computer's point of view, is one query and one IF-THEN-style comparison.

In this sketch, we've assembled a demonstration of this simple machine by using a Projected Expenditures data table. Attached to the Cost column at the right of this table is an elevator, where the carriage accumulates the various costs. This elevator carriage represents what is called in database terminology the cursor. In much the same way a visible cursor tells you where you're typing in your word processor document, a database cursor tells you which record in the data table is currently being read.

In this demonstration, the cursor carriage lifts the cost elements to the top of the elevator, where they are released and dropped into the now-familiar comparison scales. The Budget, represented by the red box in the right cup, is weighed here against the sum of the expenditures in the left cup. Below the cup is the function name SUM(expenditures), which is used in many database programming languages to refer to the total of the contents of a field or column.

PREVENTING CONFLICTS

9:20 AM
USER 1 RETRIEVES DATA FILE

9:23 AM
USER 2 RETRIEVES DATA FILE

Earlier, you saw a database being distributed among offices across continents. What happens in a multiuser, multitasking operating environment when multiple users attempt to access the same data table at roughly the same time? The sketch shows you what happens.

We begin the morning with user #1 accessing a copy of an important data table from a file maintained by the network administrator.

A few minutes later, user #2 retrieves this same file and reads the same table contents.

User #1 makes several changes to one column of the data table. He then saves the file; the changes are now recorded with the network administrator.

A few minutes later, user #2 replaces one of the records in the table. These changes have nothing to do with the column changes user #1 made earlier. Does user #2's file show the changes made by user #1?

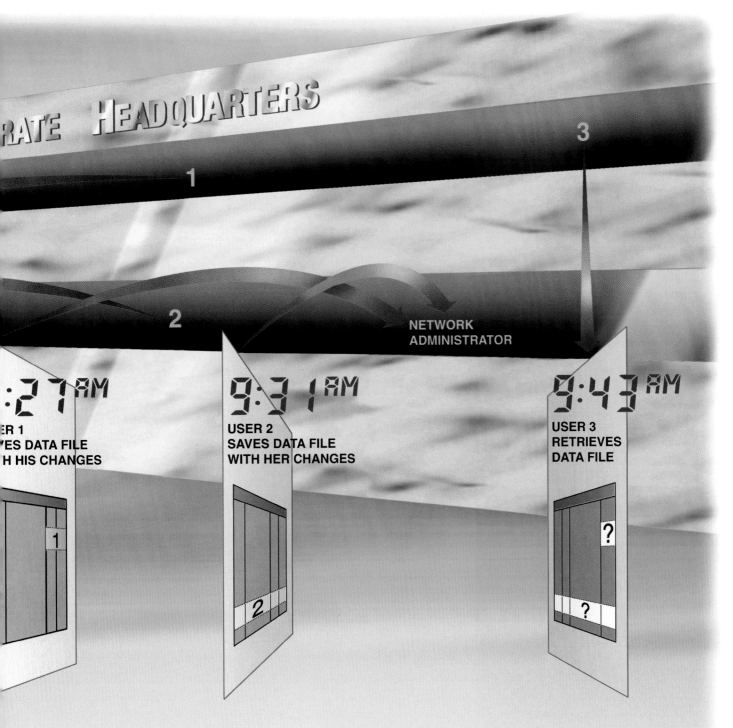

NETWORK ADMINISTRATOR

:27 AM — USER 1 SAVES DATA FILE WITH HIS CHANGES

9:31 AM — USER 2 SAVES DATA FILE WITH HER CHANGES

9:43 AM — USER 3 RETRIEVES DATA FILE

If so, when does it choose to display these changes, and how? If not, does saving #2's file undo #1's changes? What does user #3 see when he accesses the table next?

A distributed database management system must calculate precisely when changes take effect, and when to notify other users of these changes (if necessary). This way, when user #3 accesses the table later in the day, the changes made by #1 and #2 should show up, whether or not these two users are aware of each other's changes.

To prevent multiple users from accessing data at the same time, record locks are often placed on data. A record lock would prevent user #2 from accessing the same data that user #1 was updating. This forces sequential data updates rather than concurrent updates.

M HEADER

DURE HEADER

SE HEADER

SE HEADER

begin

CHAPTER 7

THE MANY WAYS TO WRITE A PROGRAM

If you've decided that you want to be a programmer, take note of the following: You do not have to learn only one high-level language. You can (and perhaps should) learn the general features of the most common high-level languages, choose your favorite, concentrate on that one, and use the others only when you have to.

Why? Because to a greater extent than you might think, high-level programming languages (especially C, C++, BASIC, and Pascal) are quite similar to one another. Most high-level languages (and by that term we mainly mean "excluding assembly language") use loop clauses and conditional clauses, and even use the same words to identify them—FOR, WHILE, and IF.

You can tell the difference between high-level languages by their *structures*—the systems within which these similar-looking clauses are used. BASIC has much looser regulations for structuring its source code than does C. As a result, the BASIC programmer has more leverage to try new processes—and maybe even see them work, however slightly flawed. On the other hand, the C programmer must create code within more strict regulations, thus creating code with fewer errors, which the compiler can interpret more quickly.

One of the common tools used by full-time professional programmers is still the assembler. There are two reasons for the assembler's continued popularity: First, although a compiler reinterprets source code into tight machine language, the programmer might know of ways to manually interpret (or translate) high-level code into tighter machine code. Second, some internal processes—such as graphics display routines—are best addressed by machine code hand-crafted by an adept programmer.

THE ASSEMBLY LANGUAGE PROGRAM

When the CPU processes a machine-language program, what does it actually *do*? Rather than show you another daunting electron microscope shot of the inside of a CPU, we've brought together some everyday objects to symbolize what a CPU spends most of its time doing. In its simplest form, a CPU compares two electrical states to generate a result. An electrical state is represented on paper by numbers; but the computer, as you saw earlier in this chapter, represents numbers as patterns of "on" and "off" bits. The CPU spends most of its time mixing "off" and "on" bits to form patterns and showing the results.

Why does the CPU compare numbers? This is the CPU's way of finding out what happens *if*—*if* a certain value is greater than it should be, *if* the buffer is running out of space, or *if* **a** is equal to **b**. Computing cannot take place unless we are constantly asking *if*. So for one of our *if*s, the CPU retrieves one number that represents the cursor location, and another that symbolizes where "the edge" of the screen is. It then performs a comparison—not to learn anything in particular about these two numbers, but instead to learn *everything* about them. The results of the comparison (such as "too much," "too little," or "out of memory") are stored in the CPU's internal *status register*.

In this sketch, the comparison takes place on a set of scales. The status register is at the top of these scales; notice the flags that wave either up or down, signaling to the computer the results of the comparison. The CPU's status register is a series of flags; you learned about them in "Binary Values as Flags" in Chapter 4.

The CPU generally receives its objects to compare from two sources. One source is *user memory*, the portion of memory (RAM) that the computer reserves for data storage while the program runs. Here is a faucet that links user memory with the scale's cup on the left. The other source is the *register*—a small cluster of memory contained within the CPU itself. It is a cabinet of sorts, where the programmer can direct certain values of high importance to be stored temporarily. A CPU contains only a handful of these registers; they're not designed, in other words, for data file storage. They have a limited amount of storage space. In our model, a crane places the contents of the index registers into the right cup.

In many CPUs, a copy of the left value in the comparison operation (written CMP in some assembly languages) is stored within the CPU's most important internal register, the *accumulator*. Many CPUs use the accumulator to hold and emphasize a particular value that is very important at the moment. The first electronic computers ever built used the accumulator register in this way. Today's CPUs use internal registers that are no longer *called* "accumulators," although that's what they are.

In short, the simple machine model shown here retrieves a value from user memory and a value from one of the index registers. It compares the two, thus setting the individual status register flags to "up" or "down" (1 or 0). The result of the comparison is stored temporarily in an internal register or accumulator. The program can then examine the status register to determine to which group of instructions the CPU should branch next. Nearly all assembly language processes involve this type of mechanism: retrieval, comparison, examination, and branching, in that order.

EGISTER

Integrating Circuitry with the Mind

The central processing unit of a computer is an extraordinarily simple machine. Even the components of the most powerful PCs made today— Intel's Pentium and Motorola's PowerPC chips—are actually easily understandable. What is so daunting about CPUs is that there are so many of these components—millions, and nearly billions—on one integrated circuit. It is the huge number of these little devices that makes the CPU work.

Assembly language gives the programmer the means of speaking directly to the CPU, with terms that the CPU immediately recognizes. There is nearly a one-to-one correlation between the lines and terms in assembly language and those in machine language (the *true* language of the CPU). Besides that, the translation process is quick, and the assembled program files are likely to be compact. The trade-off here is that the programmer must sacrifice the sentence-like constructs that make higher-level languages such as BASIC so English-like.

A high-level programming language uses terms that are phrased more like written sentences. The more a programming language resembles the way we speak and write—and at times think—the "higher" we consider that language to be. Therefore, the "highest-level" programming language possible is written language itself— English, for instance. By nature, however, English is ambiguous. Sometimes we communicate more by our tone of voice than the actual words we say. But a computer cannot "understand" what you mean when you simply say "Stop!" or "Boat?" A computer *must* follow specific rules of syntax—whether that is the syntax of C or of English.

The objective of the high-level programming language is to find some middle ground between the strict rules of machine language and the freedom of human communication. As you'll see in the next few pages, some high-level languages are higher than others. The trouble is, the higher-level languages often have more limited powers. The most powerful languages are low-level languages such as assembly language.

THE UNFULFILLED DREAM

High-level languages were inspired by the desire to write powerful code as easily as writing a grocery list. FORTRAN, COBOL, BASIC, and Pascal were conceived with the hope that eventually everyone would have access to these languages, and everyone who wanted to program *could*. The advent of mass-market applications such as

WordPerfect and 1-2-3—programs that simply plugged in and worked—was not foreseen.

The one major high-level language that escaped such inspirations altogether was C. The C language was originally designed as the programming language of the UNIX operating system. UNIX has a wide vocabulary of terms for controlling the computer—far wider than MS-DOS—but C is made available through a sort of "door" that opens up to programmers. UNIX users who weren't programmers could simply avoid the door.

Because C was "restricted," however loosely, to programmers, it could have tighter restrictions on its syntax, and therefore not cater to the amateur. C is regarded as "the language of professionals" for primarily this reason. There's really no reason why a determined amateur cannot learn C as his first programming language; but C was really designed more for the computer's benefit than for the new programmer. As you will see, this makes C one of the lowest of the high-level languages.

ADMIRAL GRACE HOPPER, FOUNDER OF COBOL

The driving force behind the creation of COBOL during the early 1960s was kept under wraps, partly due to the then-unusual fact that she was a woman. Today, she is remembered as the highest-ranking female officer in the history of the U.S. Navy. Rear Admiral Grace Hopper could be seen in the background of those early photographs of IBM's COBOL development team; her colleagues, however, knew she deserved to be up front.

During the 1970s and 1980s, Admiral Hopper became one of America's finest spokespersons on behalf of leadership training, as well as education reform. In her seminars (regardless of their intended subject matter), the Admiral explained computer concepts by using real-world objects. She would distribute to her listeners finger-length strands of copper wire, which she dubbed "nanoseconds." She explained that each strand represented the length of wire traveled by a single electron in a billionth of a second. Even in her leadership seminars, her point was for the audience to *get faster*, to start thinking of the future in tangible, visible terms and forms. Information will travel and be processed faster, but the faster it becomes, the more easily we can grasp it in our hands.

THE BASIC PROGRAM

DECLARATIONS

USER CONTROL

MAIN BODY

SUBROUTINES

Like the names of most high-level programming languages created in the 1960s, the term BASIC is an acronym—Beginner's All-Purpose Symbolic Instruction Code. BASIC was intended to be a very high-level language. MS-DOS users have a BASIC interpreter (called QBasic, BASICA, or GW-BASIC on most machines) located someplace in their \DOS directory with which they can experiment; most users aren't even aware of this fact.

The point of BASIC is to make source code easily readable by people. If a person has to use too much effort to read the source code, it isn't good BASIC.

BASIC uses sentences as a way for the programmer to tell the computer what to do; these sentences are called *instructions*. In BASIC, there are two types of instructions: A *statement* tells the computer to change something in the computer—perhaps one of the values in memory, perhaps something about the program itself. The IF-THEN conditional clause and the FOR-NEXT loop clause are both bound in BASIC by statements, because they change or affect some aspect of the program or the computer.

The other type of BASIC instruction is the *function*. When you perform any type of arithmetic or algebraic operation on a value, you perform a *function* on it. Adding another value to it is a function; squaring and cubing the value are functions. In BASIC, the programmer writes a function first by choosing which variable will hold the changed value (you learned about variables in Chapter 4), and then by writing the mathematical expression that performs the

DARTMOUTH

MICROSOFT

ANSI

change. The variable and the expression are joined together by the equal sign. A function that finds the square root of a value is thus written $x = SQR(y)$. Here, SQR is the function.

The sketch shows how BASIC programs generally are constructed. The programmer first develops the *main body* of the source code—the action of the program. He then places three layers of programming over this code. The *user control* layer contains the menus and other such devices that let the program's user tell the program what to do. The *declarations* define the initial state of the program and introduce the computer to the variables it will be using. The *subroutines* are code components, usually placed at the end, that perform some general task—such as saving a file or printing. These components may be called by the program from several locations.

There is no one single BASIC programming language. Since its introduction in 1964, there have been hundreds of derivatives of the original language, with instructions added to the vocabulary by many manufacturers—mostly without the permission of BASIC's creators.

Most BASIC interpreters currently in production can be traced back to one of three BASIC root dialects. The three root dialects of BASIC are represented in the above sketch as continents. The predominant structure was developed by Microsoft over the course of the past two decades. Microsoft's BASIC (today called QBasic or

Visual Basic) prefers nonnumbered instruction lines and Pascal-like modularity. Rather than use the GOTO and GOSUB statements for branches, Microsoft's dialect would rather you call a formally declared procedure and pass parameters to it, as you would in C.

The least predominant BASIC dialect has been issued by the American National Standards Institute (ANSI), and is used primarily by mainframe computers. This BASIC prefers that you *do* number your instruction lines (10, 20, 30, and so on) and that you declare all your variables at the beginning of the source code, rather than in separated modules.

Somewhere in between is the Dartmouth BASIC dialect, whose brand name is currently True BASIC. The creators of BASIC, the late Professor John G. Kemeny and his colleague Professor Thomas Kurtz, produced the True BASIC dialect to maintain the original structure and elegance of BASIC. True BASIC allows for branching with GOTO and GOSUB, although not in excess. It avoids modularity, under the pretext that changing terms in the midst of the source code makes that code less legible to people.

THE PASCAL PROGRAM

The inspiration behind the creation of Pascal by Professor Niklaus Wirth was that a BASIC-like language could be created almost entirely in modules. A programmer could devise working components and, once they became fully functional, enter them into any program he wrote. A True BASIC subroutine, by contrast, may require that its variable names be edited to comply with the declarations at the front of a program's source code.

Pascal uses the same For and If-Then statements as BASIC uses, although phrased slightly differently. The main difference is that Pascal was the first language to extend these statements into formal clauses, with subordinate statements that are dependent on them.

In this sketch, we've built layers that not only rest in front of one another, but oversee one another (note the overhead lamps to the right of each header representing the program and procedure headers). We've written a fragment of Pascal source code to demonstrate the types of instructions it uses. Only the variables and terms that are pertinent to the entire Pascal source code are declared within the program header; these terms are then called *global*. The rest of the source code is then divided (arbitrarily) into procedures, which are like small programs. These procedures may use their own variables and terms, called *local* because they pertain only to the procedures that declared them. One procedure may use Pascal's var declaration to declare variable x to mean one thing, and another may use var to make x mean something else entirely. This way, the programmer can import a fully functional procedure from an existing *library*, without having to change the x variable in one procedure to something else to distinguish one from another.

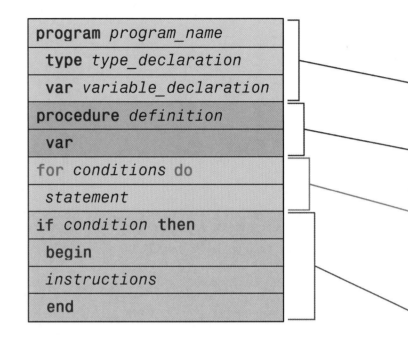

```
program program_name
  type type_declaration
  var variable_declaration
procedure definition
  var
for conditions do
  statement
if condition then
  begin
  instructions
  end
```

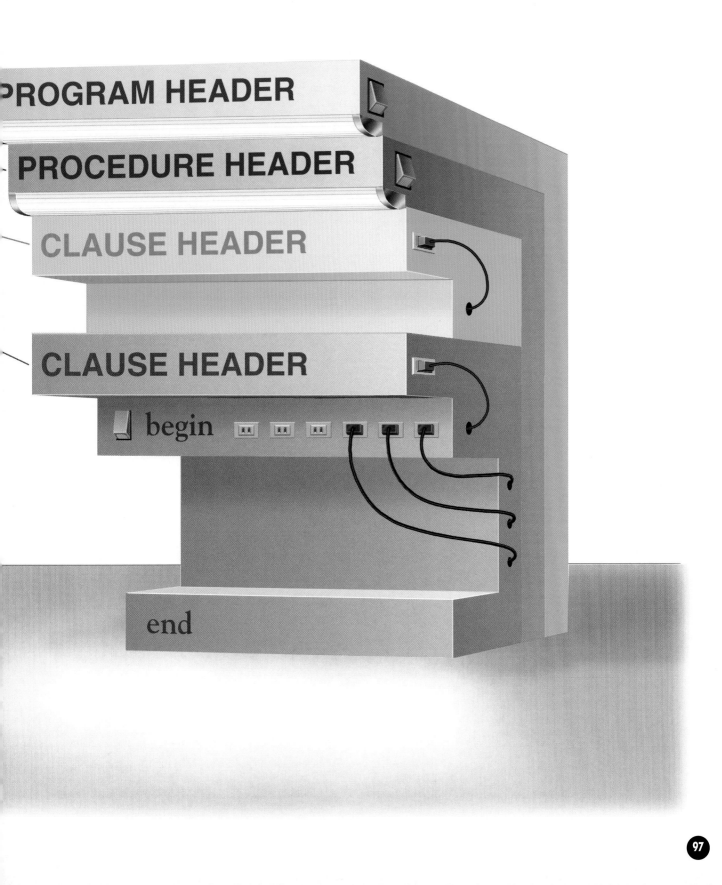

THE C PROGRAM

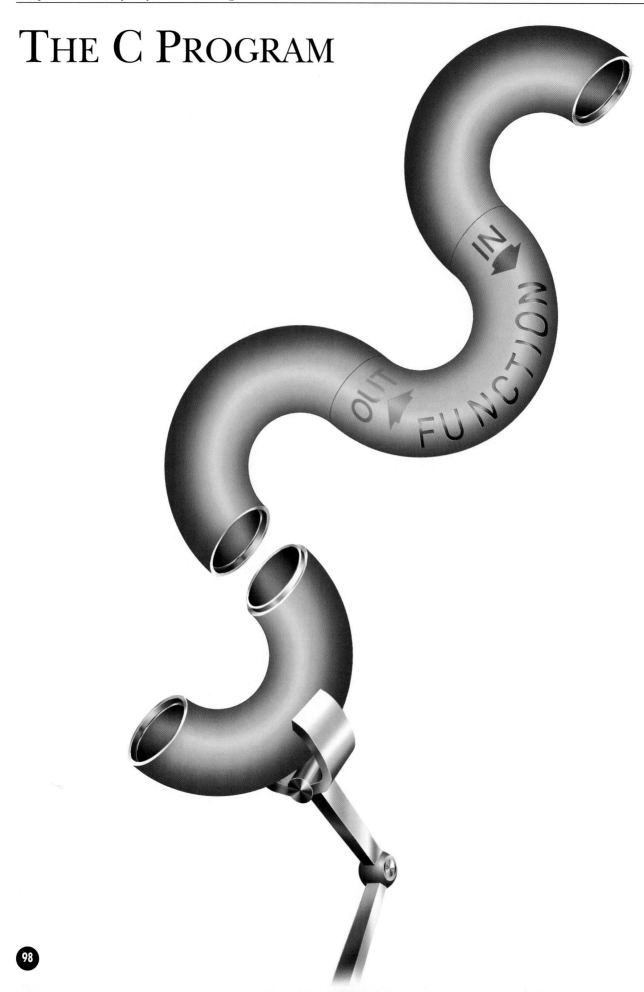

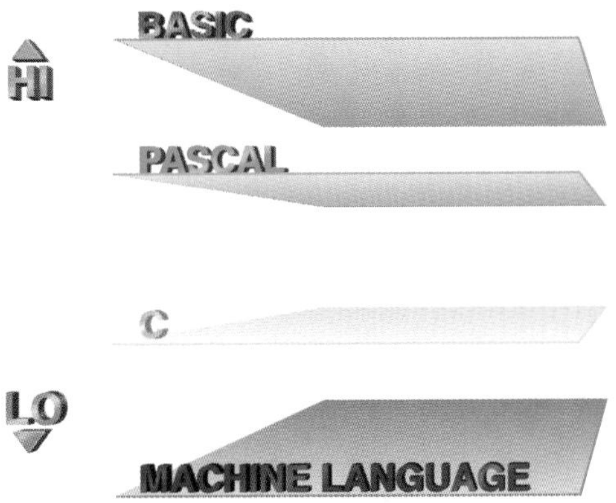

BASIC

PASCAL

C

MACHINE LANGUAGE

HI

LO

The C programming language is by far the most modular of the high-level languages. It is also the most restrictive; as this sketch shows, in some ways it is actually closer to assembly and machine language. The C program module is designed to be a fully interlocking component. It receives input values through its module header, which is made up of simply the name of the module, along with a list of the names of its input and output values. The variable names are then formally declared by first specifying the type (integer, character, binary, and so on) and then listing all those variables in the module that will use that type.

C programs are built entirely of modules that run off of the main program. These modules, represented by the elbow-shaped tubes, are linked together into a wheel, which is driven by the main module.

The goal of the professional C programmer is to be able to have nearly all of his core program components stored in advance within a special *library*, in fully working condition. To write a program for a client on short notice, this programmer may simply connect all these ready-made components. Ideally, the only C module he would then need to write from scratch is the main module, which contains the sequence of components and events.

THE COBOL PROGRAM

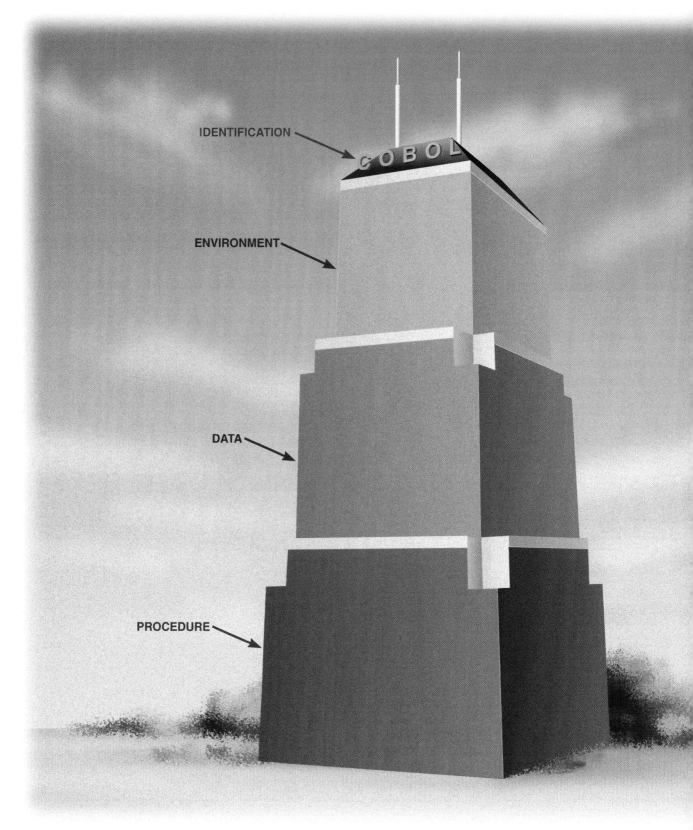

It may surprise you to learn that the high-level programming language in use today by more computers (especially minicomputers and mainframes) is not C or C++, but COBOL. The reason has to do with its age (it's older than BASIC) and how many people have it installed. Institutions with too much of an investment in older, expensive technology continue to use COBOL (*CO*mmon *B*usiness-*O*riented *L*anguage) because that is what their systems currently use, and they don't want to upgrade and just throw away their investment in existing programs. These businesses see no need to spend thousands or millions of dollars upgrading to a new system, when their current system meets their accounting and database needs.

Just because COBOL is old doesn't mean it's not an elegant language. IBM (with some help from the U.S. Defense Department) developed COBOL with the idea of making a programming language that even the newest beginner could use. The objective was to use only terminology that businesspeople already use. Some versions of COBOL use thousands of keywords, some of whose meanings even match one another. This planned redundancy was designed to correlate with the way people talk and think; we often use two or three terms in everyday language to mean the same thing.

COBOL doesn't use algebraic terms or symbols. Instead, it uses everyday words such as ADD this TO that and SUBTRACT this FROM that. It isn't exactly a modular language, but it does use clearly marked DIVISIONs. The IDENTIFICATION DIVISION distinguishes COBOL processes from one another. The ENVIRONMENT DIVISION allows the programmer to define his terms—not variables *per se*, just terms. The program's DATA DIVISION was designed to store the data or information used by the program—within the program itself; keep in mind that COBOL was created in the era of punch cards and paper tape. The PROCEDURE DIVISION, like the main module in C, defines the sequence of events; what is done, in what order, and what specifically is done in the program.

CHAPTER 8

THE ARCHITECTURE OF PROGRAMMING

It's been said that the most intimidating thing an author faces each day is the blank page. An author best fills that space not with mere words, but ideas. A programmer stares at a blank screen every day. Rather than imagine the screen filled with lines and lines of as-yet-unrealized source code, the professional programmer visualizes ideas.

But just what is it that he *sees*? It's relatively easy to convey a thought or a concept with an ordinary sentence, but what about a process? Writing a computer program is not like giving explicit directions to someone about how to organize the file cabinet or fix the gutters on the side of the house.

A computer is virtually as dumb as a sledgehammer. The programmer's job is to teach this blunt instrument to balance a checkbook, for instance; but here's the catch: The programmer cannot be specific about which checkbook. The application must be able to balance *any* checkbook, regardless of its content. Consequently, the application must be taught the *theory* of checkbook balancing, not just the process; and the programmer starts with *nothing*. How does an electronic device, with no real understanding of the world at large, become informed about the theoretical nature of a real-world process? The answer has to do entirely with simple *symbols*, as you'll see in the next few pages.

THE ROLE OF FLOWCHARTING

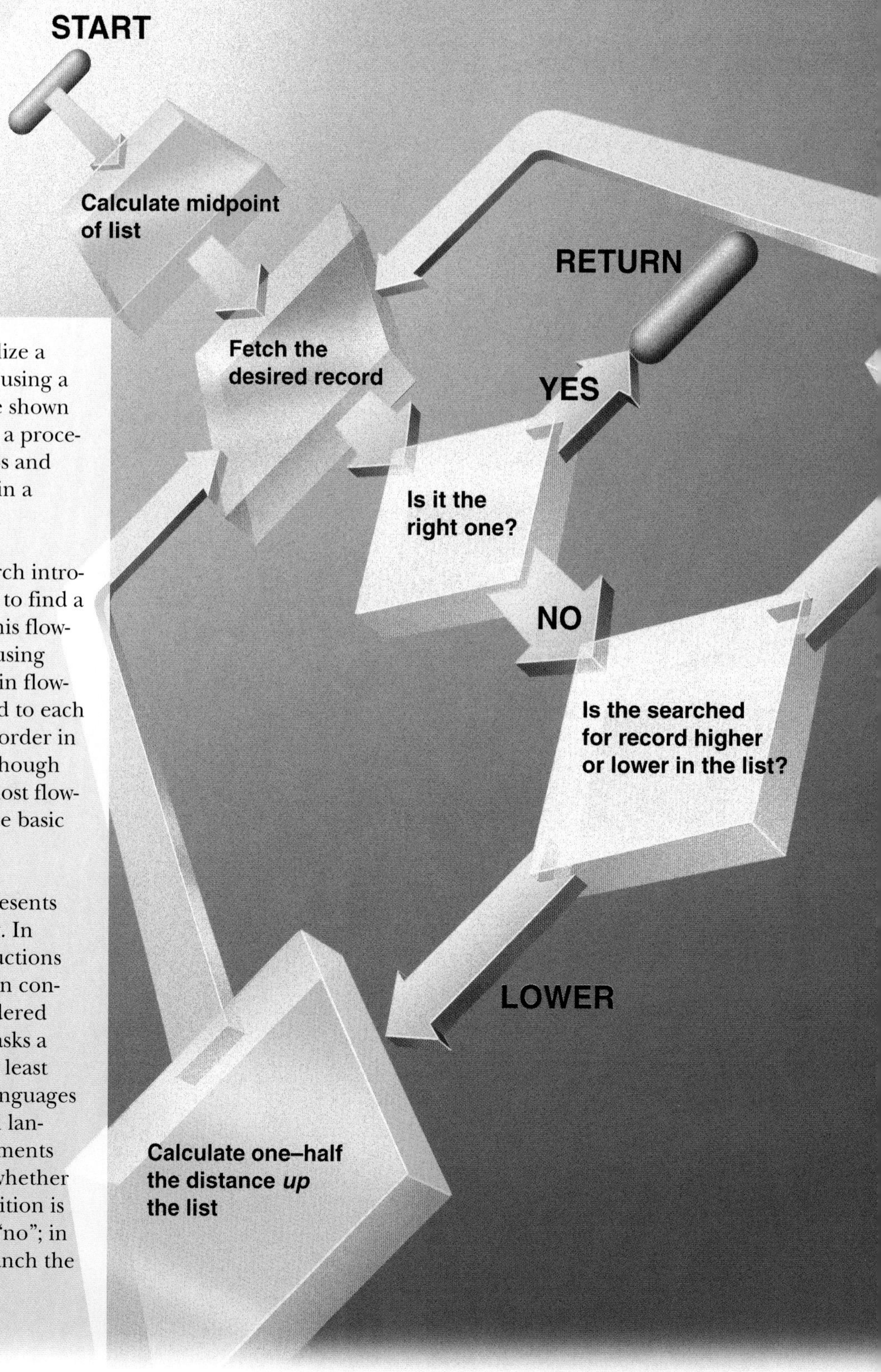

START

Calculate midpoint of list

Fetch the desired record

RETURN

YES

Is it the right one?

NO

Is the searched for record higher or lower in the list?

LOWER

Calculate one–half the distance *up* the list

S ome programmers visualize a real-world procedure by using a *flowchart*, such as the one shown here. A flowchart breaks a procedure into individual steps and categorizes each step by placing it in a specific shape.

You may remember the binary search introduced in Chapter 5, whose job was to find a specific entry in a presorted list. This flowchart shows that same procedure, using three of the most common shapes in flowcharting. The shapes are connected to each other with arrows, which show the order in which each shape is to be read. Although there is no one way to flowchart, most flowcharting systems today use the three basic shapes shown at right.

The rectangle, nicknamed DO, represents a step that must be performed now. In programming languages, the instructions represented by a DO rectangle (often containing the calculations) are considered *statements*. The IF diamond always asks a question, for which there can be at least two answers. Low- and high-level languages both use IF instructions. High-level languages, as you've seen, use IF statements within a conditional clause to test whether some condition is true. An IF condition is generally answered with a "yes" or "no"; in this flowchart, the IF diamonds branch the flowchart in two directions.

The GET parallelogram represents a data acquisition process, or what SQL database programmers call a *fetch*. Reading a record into memory from a data file is one process represented by a GET shape. This particular flowchart uses an IBM convention: Capsule shapes represent the beginning and the end of the flowchart procedure.

Here's how to read this flowchart: Beginning at START, the first arrow leads you to the first DO rectangle, which reads, "Calculate midpoint of list." Notice there are no "*ifs*" about this process; the computer is simply to shut up and do it. Next comes the GET shape, which represents reading a record from the file.

At the first IF diamond, check to see whether the acquired record is the one you're looking for. If it is, the arrow marked YES leads you directly to the end of the procedure. The NO arrow takes you to the next IF test, "Is the searched-for record higher or lower in the list?" Either the HIGHER or LOWER arrow takes the procedure to another DO rectangle, telling the procedure to move the record pointer up or down the list by half the distance of the last jump. Notice how the arrows on both sides lead back to the GET shape; this looping back upward symbolizes exactly that, a *loop*.

Calculate one–half the distance *down* the list

R

THE MEANING IN THE OBJECT

In Chapter 2, in a panel titled, "What It Means to Be Object-Oriented," you saw that modern applications manage data in the form of complex constructs called *objects*. The difference between an object and an ordinary data record is that an ordinary record has meaning only to the person reading it, but an object has meaning to the computer also.

A complex object contains instructions that define how that object works; so when the programmer tells it to go work, the object may then perform the instructions it was given. This changes the contents of the data record being maintained by that object. An object alters its own contents in response to written instructions *contained within it*; an ordinary record, by contrast, must be altered manually by way of instructions contained *outside* that record.

You can compare the function of data objects to an aircraft in flight. Assume that the application you're writing is an air traffic control simulator. The ordinary data for an aircraft that you'd keep in a data file may include the name and the owner of the aircraft, its destination, and how many people are on board. This information may be pertinent to the air traffic controller, but certainly less so than its compass heading and its velocity. This is crucial information that probably needs to be formally stored at some time; but just how functional would an air control tower be if it worked like a database manager: SELECT all_aircraft FROM sky WHERE headed = crash?

Call Sign	Airline	Jet Type	Final Destin
DTA 962	Dallas	MD-11	Housto
AR 141	Astral	727	San Anto

Objective-AIRCR

ource	Complement
tlanta	153
emphis	91

Altitude	Bearing	Heading	Velocity
3350	35	170	45
2735	181	335	39

DATA

plane. GO()

Programmers have found that the most efficient way to maintain data that might change is as objects, which are supported only by certain high-level languages such as C++ and Object Pascal. An object for this simulator instructs the symbolic plane—just a blip on the radar—how and where to move. The plane object's internal data is changed accordingly.

So if an airplane object in a simulator application is instructed how to "go," it can be "trained" to respond to a simple programmer-defined directive, such as DO. If it's time for the program to make the plane move, the programmer may simply write plane.GO().

Here's where something called *object classification* becomes very important: If there's more than one plane in the air, the source code may classify them all as one group, by giving them a common *class* called planes. Each member of the class may have a slightly different way to respond to the command GO(); but if they all recognize that same term, the source code can move all the planes in the sky with the statement planes.GO(). To take this one step further, if the simulator deals with planes, trains, and automobiles, the source code could make them all move with the statement vehicles.GO(). Each vehicle covered by the simulator first has to be classified under vehicles; but then, they could all be programmed to respond either separately or jointly.

Making It Go

All programs are structures. This is partly why programmers say that there is an "architecture" to programming. Any professional architect knows that the core element of every building, bridge, and skyscraper is its underlying simple structure. Any engineer knows that the most durable structure in nature is the simplest structure.

So the programmer who stares at the blank screen doesn't just jump in blindly, design step one, and go where fancy leads. He first imagines the *end product*—how this application will work when it's completed. He then works backward toward the beginning, breaking down the components of the design in his mind until he comes across step one. This breakdown is a *simplification* of the seemingly complex to the devastatingly simple. A computer, after all, is not a complex tool; it only "knows" how to jam together two electrical states and see what comes out the other end.

This situation leads to one of the key rules of the art of programming: If you cannot simplify it, you should not program it.

WHY OBJECTIFY?

Whereas a data record maintains the relative state of something being represented in the database, an object defines—again relatively—what that something does. You've seen how an application's source code uses variables to act as the containers for important values. A data record in memory is maintained with a set of variables. The computer may be instructed to alter this record, but the record isn't any more aware of this alteration than a year-old family portrait is aware of what the family did since that portrait was taken. A record is a snapshot of the state of something.

An object uses variables to represent—moreover, to *symbolize*—important values, just like a data record. It also uses mathematical expressions and high-level statements to symbolize *changes* in those values, and how those changes are to take place. Without objects, every change that the computer is to make to a data record must be explicitly specified. With objects, this change is given a name: a *verb*. The source code invokes the verb, and the object responds to its name. Because we recognize real-world objects not only for what they are but also for what they do, it can only be simpler to recognize computerized objects not only for their relative state, but also for their relative change.

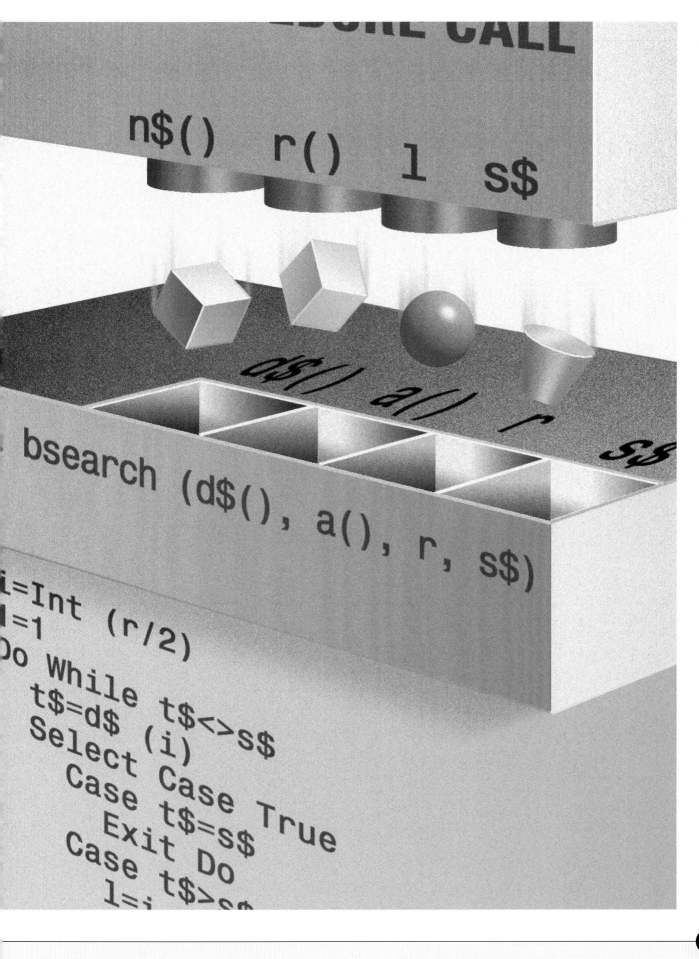

```
n$()  r()  l  s$
```

```
d$()  a()  r  s$
```

```
bsearch (d$(), a(), r, s$)
i=Int (r/2)
l=1
Do While t$<>s$
  t$=d$ (i)
  Select Case True
    Case t$=s$
      Exit Do
    Case t$>s$
      l=i
```

MODULAR CONSTRUCTION

In "Finding Order in Modules" in Chapter 2, you saw some ordinary household objects arranged on a basketball court, in a loose but effective demonstration of how the average module works. In this sketch is a real module, the search algorithm as written in Microsoft's modern QBasic dialect. Here is the flowchart from a few pages back, demonstrating how the instructions in the QBasic module are reflected in the flowchart.

The procedure header at the top of the module shows that your search algorithm is named bsearch, which is short for "binary search." In the parentheses are four input variables. The first two variables represent arrays. The open-and-closed parentheses () help symbolize array variables in BASIC, whereas the dollar sign $ shows that the variable represents words (what BASIC calls "strings") rather than numerical values.

For the purposes of this function module, array variable d$() contains the list of names being searched. Array variable a() acts as a pointer to the data records stored on disk that d$() maintains in memory. Variable r tells how many records there are in the list, wheras string variable z$ contains the name for which the module is looking.

The values for these four input variables are supplied by an outside procedure. The particular procedure shown by the bar at top has named all four of these variables differently, except for z$. Nonetheless, while these values are visiting this function module, they are represented by the names given them in the bsearch procedure header.

The first two instructions in the module establish the location of the first record to be searched, in the exact middle of the array. The loop clause here is bound by the Do While... statement at top, and the Loop statement just above the close of the module. Every instruction between these two statements is to be executed While t$<>s$ (while the name you've found t$ is not equal to the name you're looking for, s$). Inside the module, variable i represents the record number you're currently looking at, so the term d$(i) means the record in array d$ that is numbered i.

In QBasic, the Select Case conditional clause tests for multiple possibilities; in this instance, you're looking for which of the following tests is True. If you've found the name you're looking for Case t$=s$, you can exit the loop clause now (Exit Do). If your name falls before the name you're looking at (Case t$<s$), the computer is to calculate half the distance of the last jump *up* the list (the first jump being half the length of the entire list). The final Case is obviously the reverse of the previous one, having the computer jump halfway *down* the list.

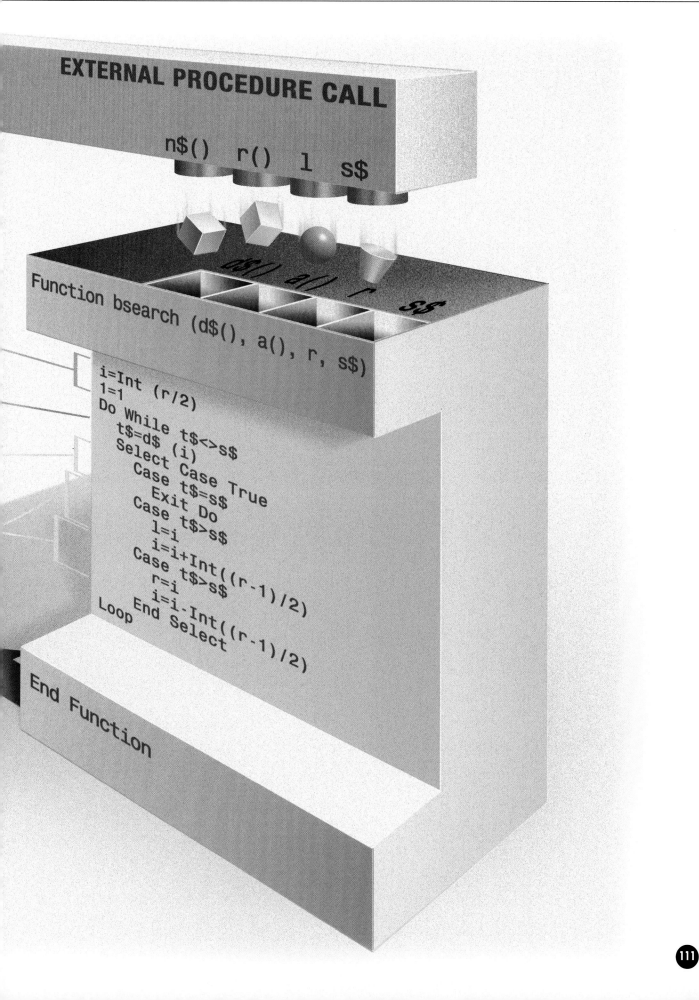

EXTERNAL PROCEDURE CALL

n$()   r()   l   s$

Function bsearch (d$(), a(), r, s$)

```
i=Int (r/2)
1=1
Do While t$<>s$
    t$=d$ (i)
    Select Case True
        Case t$=s$
            Exit Do
        Case t$>s$
            1=i
            i=i+Int((r-1)/2)
        Case t$>s$
            r=i
            i=i-Int((r-1)/2)
    End Select
Loop
```

End Function

111

WHERE TO MOUNT THE ENGINE

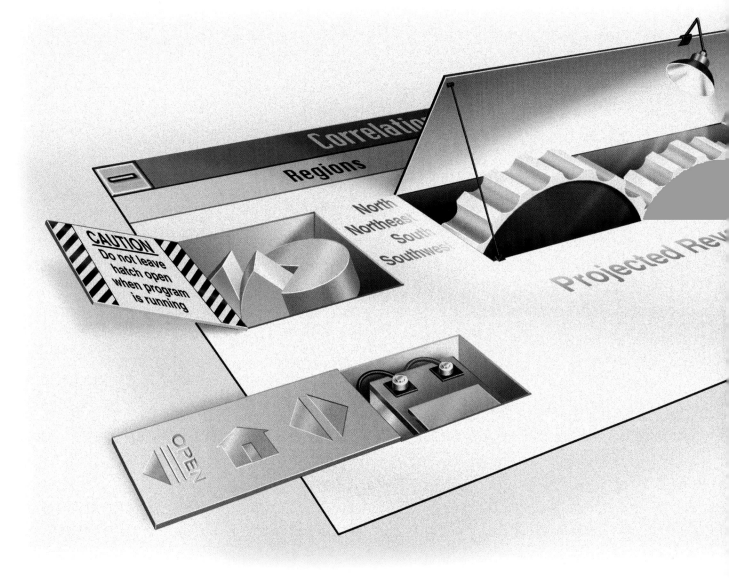

The core element of any application is a simple process, what programmers call "the engine." As you've seen, you can sketch a simple process by using a flowchart. Using flowcharts, you discover that all the other procedures encompassed by an application become secondary to the main process.

But what is that main process? In "The Application Model" in Chapter 1, you learned that the professional programmer generally develops the arithmetic and data processing features first. Yet is this always the case? Suppose you were writing a graphics illustrator application. The main element of this application, it would seem, would be the use of the drawing tools. On the surface, this appears to be a problem of developing the "user model," the methods for how the user is to operate this program.

The deeper problem, you come to realize, is that of how your application is going to represent the user's drawing in memory. There's no real way of testing the user operation features until some part of your program can actually draw—until black ink shows up on a white page. So you need to develop an image format, at least as far as memory is concerned.

Still, there's no way of testing the long-term viability of the drawing format until you have a working pencil and a toolbox to put that pencil in. So does the pencil come before the drawing? Some would argue that it does, that an application must first be made workable before it can be made to work. Practice teaches the professional, however, that a workable shell is no good without a working engine; and furthermore, that the nature of the working engine defines the shape and function of the shell.

As this drawing shows, the shell is drawn and *looks* good, but it is not usable until the underlying engine and parts are properly working. The shell can only carry the product so far; at some point the user will actually try to use the product and see that it is an empty shell.

WRITING THE DIALOGUE BETWEEN PROGRAMS

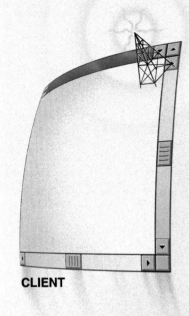

CLIENT

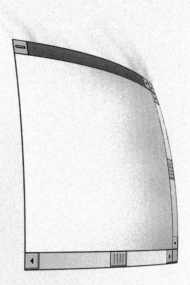

OS

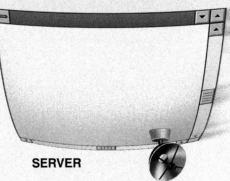

SERVER

DATA

Today, the buyer or the client expects an application to be able to share data with other applications. Sharing data requires some degree of communication between applications. On many computing platforms, including Microsoft Windows, IBM OS/2, and the Apple System, sharing requires something similar to *telecommunication.*

These platforms borrow a concept from modern PC networking called the *client/server model.* In this model, shown above, an application has to "want" another application's data before sharing can take place. It then "broadcasts" a message that it wants data; this signal is either picked up by the operating system (OS) and passed on, or passed from program to program in search of an answerer. Eventually, the signal is picked up by an application capable of fulfilling this request.

The recipient application responds by transmitting an acknowledgment signal. Again, this is a sort of "broadcast" message, because most platforms do not yet support individual pipelines between applications. Every program in the environment is tuned into the conversation between these two applications; nothing is private.

Now that a conversation exists (however public), you can refer to the caller application as the *client* and the respondent as the *server*. The server will fulfill the request and supply the desired data. First, there's a series of "hello" signals called *handshaking*. What takes place next is not a handoff of the data from program to program; remember, there is no pipeline here. The requested data exists in memory someplace, and cannot be moved by an application; only the operating system can move data. The server can tell the client, however, where this data is located by relating its memory address. The client may then access the data at that location, whenever it's ready.

The communication channels between applications on UNIX platforms are far more *segregated* than on PC environment platforms. The reason has to do with *shared memory*. With Windows, OS/2, and the Apple System, data is the product of one application, and therefore is considered to "belong" to that application, even if it's written in an object-oriented format. Sharing, therefore, is a matter of passing control of this data from one application to another, if only temporarily.

On UNIX platforms, applications have their own private memory allocations, although they also have public space where their real products are being developed. Three applications whose assignments concern different aspects of the same items, therefore, may share the same data without asking each other's permission. For instance, a computer session being run at NASA concerning the Hubble space telescope may involve three applications, represented below as Design, Accounting, and Simulation. After changes are made to the construction of the telescope by Design, the projected costs can automatically be changed by Accounting, and those same changes can be incorporated within Simulation. These three applications are indeed aware of each other's presence; as long as the object-oriented telescope data is available to all three at all times, however, little needs to be said between them.

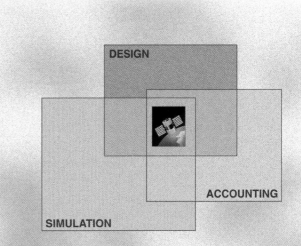

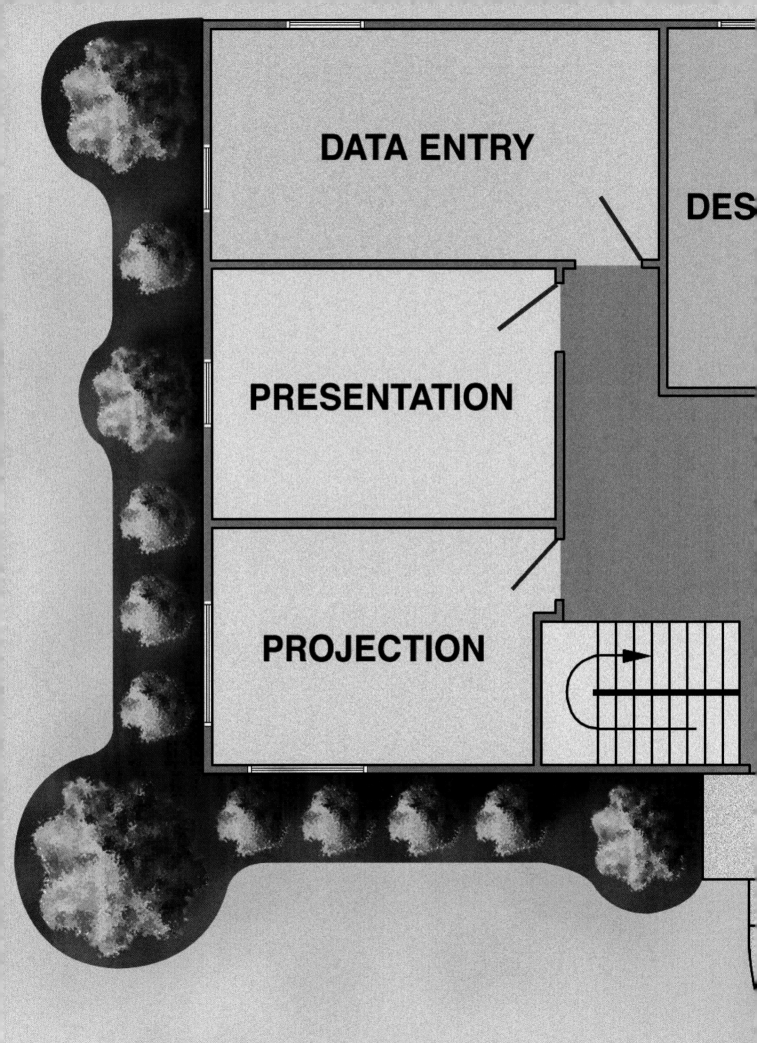

CHAPTER 9

HOW A
PROGRAMMER
THINKS

An automobile designer's mission is to find either a suitable container to hold the car's engine as it moves along the road, or a suitable engine to move the chassis. A computer programmer has a similar goal: to either develop a functional model to contain a perfect process, or to conceive a process best suited to drive the new and (hopefully) innovative user interface.

The program code and user interface of an application are like the engine and chassis of an automobile. The program code generally takes precedence if for historical reasons alone; without an engine, what's the point of building the machine? By the same measure, no one would spend hours designing the shell of an accounting program if he couldn't design the needed formulas.

But as in the case of Dan Bricklin, the inventor of the spreadsheet, the goal of some programmers is to develop a functional and economical engine that will justify the need for their ideal user interface. Arguably, the computer's real role in the workplace is to present a more functional, reasonable way to work. Someone has to design and redefine how work is done. The spreadsheet application facilitated entirely new forms of computing processes, which were unforeseen before Bricklin's idea.

You could debate about "Which comes first, the program code or the interface?" In either event, the programmer creates a new way to work every time he develops an application. Whether that new way to work is *reasonable* for the user remains to be seen. How is it that a programmer envisions a new work procedure, reinventing the wheel each time? Not all programmers think alike; by looking at the most successful programmers, however, you can see how the programmer's thought process *should* proceed.

ENVISIONING THE APPLICATION

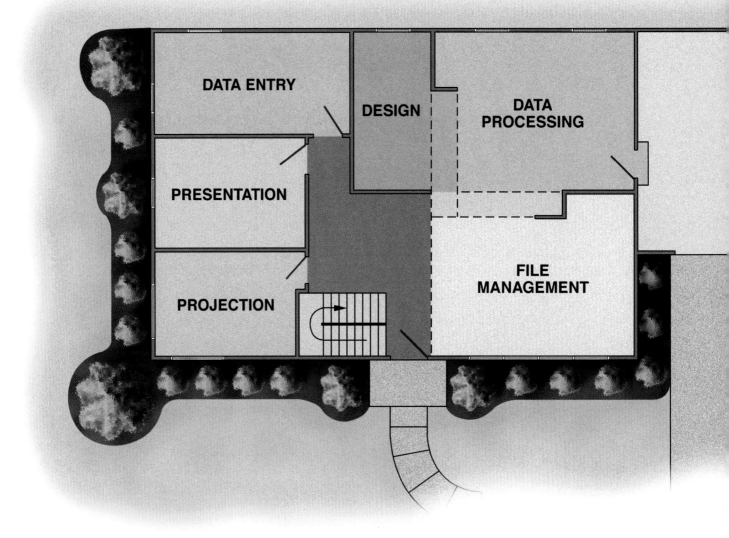

Ahouse is a functional unit of space. When you consider moving into a new house, you examine the floorplan or layout of its rooms, and imagine the flow of everyday life among those rooms. Does it really make sense, for example, for the laundry room to be located upstairs? Because all the dirty clothes are gathered upstairs anyway, perhaps so. On the other hand, this arrangement may make the entire upper floor vibrate regularly to the sound of the machine.

The division of functions in a computer application should be like the division of rooms in a house. An application is a multi-function program, and the user spends a great deal of session time going from one function of the application to another. Part of the purpose of graphical computing is to give the functions of an application the *appearance* of location. This way, the user feels familiar with the interface.

Here is a "blueprint" in which the various functions of an all-purpose application are divided among the various "rooms." Related

Lotus Development Corp. and headed the design team that produced *1-2-3*, introduced the house blueprint analogy explored here. In it, Kapor points out that, in searching for elements of good home design, you first consult an architect rather than an engineer, because the arrangement of rooms (functions) is far more important in people's minds than wiring and plumbing. Functions with related purposes, he stated, should be arranged near to one another, not separately as other models had chosen thus far. Designing an application around its user interface, Kapor stated further, would be like designing a new automobile around a cool idea for a dashboard. Good design philosophy gives precedence to a powerful and economic engine, from which you then give the driver sensible and ergonomic access to the power from that engine.

functions are nearer to one another; the arrangement is not arbitrary. There is no best way to arrange the rooms in such a blueprint (after all, the shape of your "house" was arbitrary), although the point of the blueprint concept is to aid the programmer in arranging related elements.

The term "architecture" has been used with regard to computer program design for some time. In his 1990 Software Design Manifesto, **Mitch Kapor** formally proposed that, like drafting, programming requires some visual design. Kapor, who founded

Converting an Everyday Task into a Program

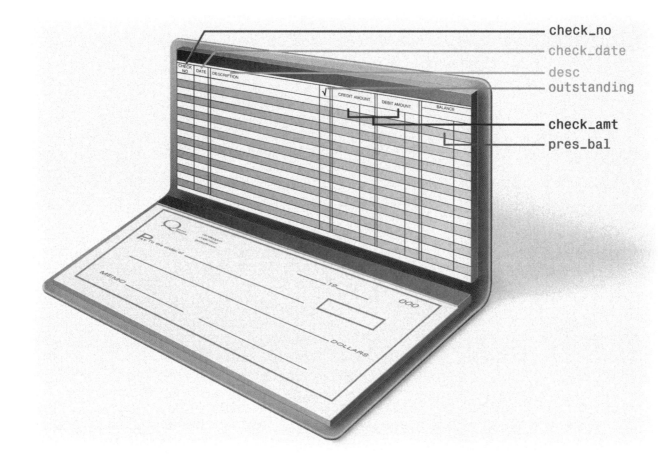

Every time a programmer creates a new application, he invents a new way to work. This new way, however, should not be so different from the *old* way that it requires more time or effort. On the other hand, if the computer's way to work is equivalent to the old way to work, the computer has added nothing new to the process.

A delicate balance must be maintained in the design of an application that models an ordinary process, such as checkbook balancing. There really is no better way to balance a checkbook than to add together all the numbers; but this is what people have the most trouble doing. People purchase a checkbook-balancing application, for the most part, to take care of the simple, everyday process of addition; however, a calculator can do that just as well. What the computer should do is add some *visibility* to the process—show the user what's really going on with his expenditures.

To model the real process, you start with the real thing. Every checkbook has its own "database," so it's easy to isolate the variables that relate to the important elements of check writing. The drawing on the left shows the variables the programmer has selected. From here, the programmer develops a form that simplifies the data entry process (the finished check, right); naturally, a check should look something like a check, even if oversimplified.

The real "engine" of this application, however, is its reporting. The application should be able to show what's happening on a day-by-day basis. From there, the programmer can add an important functional layer, budgeting. Now the application has a real purpose: allowing the user to plan, and see whether the present status of his accounts meets that plan. The simplest type of report for the user to interpret (and the most difficult to implement) involves graphics. Lines that go up or down tell the user much more in a shorter time than bunches of digits in columns. Now, the application has actually added something to the checkbook process, first by automating the process, and next by adding functionality and providing a new way to view the information.

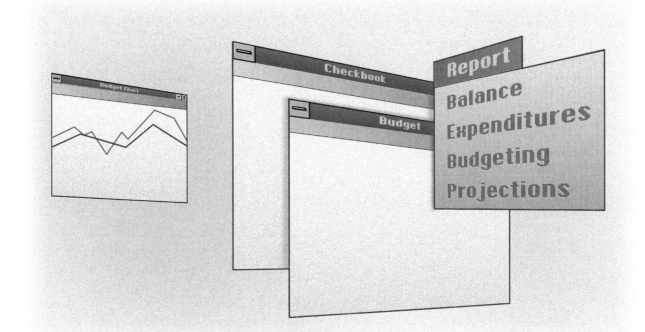

In Search of Sensibility

The programmers who work for software corporations are faced with a nearly impossible task. Their job is to write an application that supports the features of its operating system (OS), to a level desired by the marketing division of the manufacturer of that OS. At the same time, the OS's features seem to change almost weekly.

Microsoft, IBM, and Apple each have their own standards for *inter-application communication*—exchanging data between applications. Although standards exist specifying how applications on the same platform should communicate, not much is said about precisely what these applications are to say to one another. But adequate support of the platform must be there for the application to earn the coveted support logo of its OS—and to display this logo on its packaging.

The application must support the new database and object-orientation standards that the OS manufacturers are developing. This means the data produced by the application must be arranged and delimited (marked with "fenceposts") in a manner specified by the OS, using this week's version of the standard. Other applications sharing the same OS and environment then can use this data. What the other application is supposed to be able to *do* with this data is probably a matter for the developer of that other application.

Or is it? Apple, Microsoft, and IBM have asked their OS developers to form coalitions to build an inter-application language that allows one application not only to give object data to another application, but also to be able to tell that other application what that data is for. In all three cases, the developers either drew a blank, or failed to work well together in the first place. The three corporations then took it on themselves to create or use their own inter-application language standards. Apple has developed and is revising AppleEvents as a way to give programs on the Macintosh and other Apple OSs their own parts of speech. Microsoft is developing a language system based on its popular Visual Basic programming language; and IBM is using a system called AREXX that first came to microcomputers from the Commodore Amiga.

THE TROUBLE WITH WRITING AN APPLICATION THAT CAN PORT OPERATING SYSTEMS

So in the face of all these muffled languages and corporate politics, how does a programmer envision a working application? He does it by creating a conceptual model—the same thing you've done throughout this book to visualize the components of a program in a totally abstract manner.

An application being designed to support all the major OSs is first *drawn* before it is written. Some programmers use flowcharts for this purpose, others their own "drafting tools." The purpose here, to borrow again from Mitch Kapor, is to concentrate on the design of the engine and a component chassis, without having to be concerned at first with support for all the different graphic interface shells. C++ has become the development language of choice among professionals because nothing about it is operating system-specific. The OSs do attempt to place their stamp on the language; but for the most part, a C++ program works as well on one OS as it does on another.

The C++ programming language was developed originally for use with UNIX. As its name implies, UNIX was designed for universality, to make the functionality of both the system and its applications equivalent to one another across all computer OSs. In that same spirit, in the early 1980s the Massachusetts Institute of Technology developed an interapplication environment for UNIX, called X. The graphical form of that environment is X Windows. It is owned by no one, and is presented as a way to give all applications some graphical universality and uniformity, much like C gives to source code. There are several implementations of X Windows—Open Look and OSF/Motif are most prominent among them—but because they follow the X standard, an application running on Open Look runs just as easily on Motif. They'll *look* slightly different, but they will be the same program, because their graphical features follow the standards of X. The X Windows toolkit and OSF/Motif are both maintained by an organization called X/Open.

Professional programmers on other OSs are beginning to use X Windows as a model for themselves, even though their applications may never be ported to UNIX. UNIX is an OS where universality, like it or not, works. The goal of professional programmers is to write applications that can be implemented on a Macintosh and on a Pentium computer with little or no change to the source code. X-like functionality may be a role model for this new form of platform-generic programming.

REDUCING A PROCESS TO ITS SIMPLEST FORM

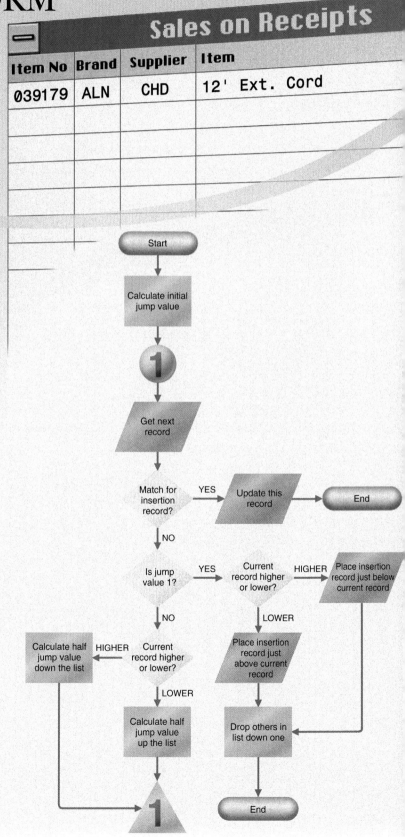

In algebra, you learn to take a formula and *reduce* it, so that it performs the same function with the fewest terms. A programmer-for-hire has to perform similar reductions every day; but how does he accomplish this when the nature of his projects changes so often?

Here's an ordinary job a programmer may be hired to perform for a client: build an engine for reading and analyzing sales figures for a hardware store. The store isn't yet computerized, so all its sales figures are currently stored on bunches of invoice receipts torn off the tape of the cash register. After the program is written, each sale must be entered into the application by hand.

At right is a flowchart showing one "engine" process for entering a receipt-tape entry into a database. This chart is modeled after the search flowchart you saw earlier in the

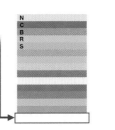

But wait! Some of these receipts contain returns for refund. These entries are listed here, and must be entered into the computer as negative sales values. Such a situation may end up removing an entry from the middle of the Top 10 list, making the others below it move up to fill the gap. When that happens, #10 becomes #9; but where does the new #10 come from?

The sales figures are cumulative totals, which are important only at the end of the data entry process. So perhaps you don't need a Top 10 list after all. You could instead create an *index* that points to certain entries in the cumulative table and allows the program to more easily generate those sales totals at the end. Each entry in the index points to the location of the entry in the main data table; and because index entries are smaller, they're easier to maintain as well as to access.

book. The idea here is that the database will contain the cumulative sales of all items; so an item that you find on the receipt may already appear in the database. The engine must search for that entry first. If it doesn't exist, the engine creates a new entry. Here is a new flowchart feature from the IBM standard: The circle and triangle, both marked "1," represent the contents of a loop. The loop starts at circle 1, and continues until it reaches triangle 1. From there, the flow jumps back up to circle 1.

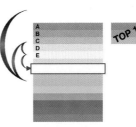

The engine searches first for a match for the existing entry. It "knows" no such entry exists when the "jump value" (the number of entries the internal pointer is to be moved next) is already set to 1 and can no longer be divided in half. When that happens, an entry is added to the table at the current location, thus keeping the data table sorted at all times.

As long as you have a sorted index, why do you need a sorted main table now? Perhaps you can store each new entry at the end after all, and just keep the index sorted as you go. The problem becomes one of redundancy. In an unsorted main table of receipts, are multiple entries for any one item; thus it becomes necessary to have just as many entries in the sorted index. This makes the index practically pointless, because the values it is indexing are no longer unique; it's like having an alphabet with five or six letter "Rs."

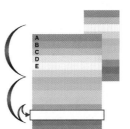

Is a constantly sorted data table necessary to the program? After all, you won't be reading the sales results until after all the receipts have been tallied. It may be more economical to enter each entry at the bottom of the list and sort the list later. In the meantime, the program simply maintains an unsorted list, represented here by the table at top right. How does the programmer determine the answer to this dilemma?

The most economical solution to the problem doesn't involve indexes at all: Put entries into an unsorted table. Sort them at the end of data entry, and then create an algorithm to combine all the similar items into one entry, because they'll all be next to one another, anyway.

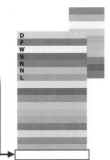

Because the receipts eventually will show the same item purchased twice, it is necessary to keep a constantly sorted list, using the insertion engine flowcharted on the left page. Along the way, the program could maintain a Top 10 Sales chart, with entries that sold more being placed ahead of others.

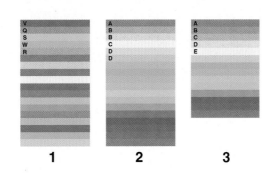

1   2   3

WHAT EXPERIENCE TEACHES THE PROGRAMMER

The solution to one problem may not work for another problem. The same methodology most likely will not work for any and all applications. Suppose the programmer is working on an application for tracking the process of stocks in a portfolio, in *real-time* (as events happen). The application takes stock trading values as they appear on the ticker. Each listing on the ticker is added to a cumulative portfolio table. The application's objective is first to help the trader determine his current portfolio value, second to spot trends immediately, and third to determine what to buy, how, and when.

Here's the problem: Stocks to *buy* aren't always stocks that appear in the portfolio; so the application will have to keep track of the entire stock exchange. Along the way, the application will accumulate the Top 10 sellers, winners, and losers—although there are several different ways to determine what's winning and what's losing. A stock traded on the New York exchange (NYSE), for instance, may have lost several points in dollar value; but if the trading volume was relatively low, this may not be entirely bad news—just a momentary reaction to a bad economic report.

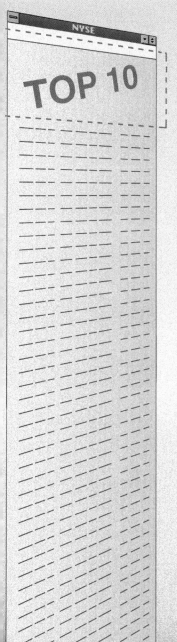

So there are many different formulas for trends and totals that the stock application needs to execute. When, however, will it find time to execute them? The ticker runs from the beginning of trade to the close without stopping. Perhaps the application can do what the CPU does in a computer: use a buffer. Modern stock tickers run at about 16 characters per second. In the time it takes a modern computer to accumulate 16 characters, it could perform countless analyses.

The application, therefore, has to maintain some type of regulator, telling it when to stop and examine the 16 characters in its per-second buffer. This regulator isn't difficult to program; in fact, the flowchart for it appears below. The purple parallelogram represents the acquisition of a character. The yellow diamond represents the test for 16. If it's 16, flush the buffer into a variable; if not, keep reading.

The string variable contains all the noninterpreted characters from the ticker; there will probably be one or two leftover characters from the previous second. Once a trade is interpreted, it is inserted into the huge NYSE database, using the insertion method profiled in "Reducing a Process to Its Simplest Form." Now, you could just sort this NYSE list according to one analysis formula rather than alphabetically, and skim the Top 10 off the top. This is an option, although we'd probably need a separate alphabetic index to point the insertion engine to the location of an entry to be updated. Again, what appears at first to be a simplification is actually a complication. It's probably better to have the stock application assess the Top 10s during the gaps between seconds.

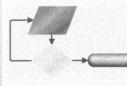

PROJECTING HOW THINGS WILL GO WRONG

I n any computer process, even those that work flawlessly as far as source code is concerned, something will go wrong. The user may make a mistake, the environment may misalign the pointer to your active data file, or the application can do everything right and still disappoint the user.

Above is one such problem that may occur: Suppose that during the process of entering those receipt tape values for the program profiled in "Reducing a Process to Its Simplest Form," one of the receipts shows that a customer returned an item for which there is no history of him ever buying. Suddenly there's an entry for this nonexistent item selling –1 units; so numerically speaking, this is the worst-selling item ever. A well thought-out application watches for such entries and skims them from the top of the Worst Sellers list. However, this receipt involves a real transaction, so it cannot be simply removed from the cumulative table.

On the bottom left is a common problem that results from the computer's sorting mechanism on a list of names. Every computer represents numbers and characters as an ASCII code number. A is "less than" Z because it falls before it in the ASCII code. The problem sets in when you see that a left quotation mark falls below A in that same code. So a book that for all practical purposes begins with the letter *S* might show up at the top of a sorted book list if the first character is a punctuation mark.

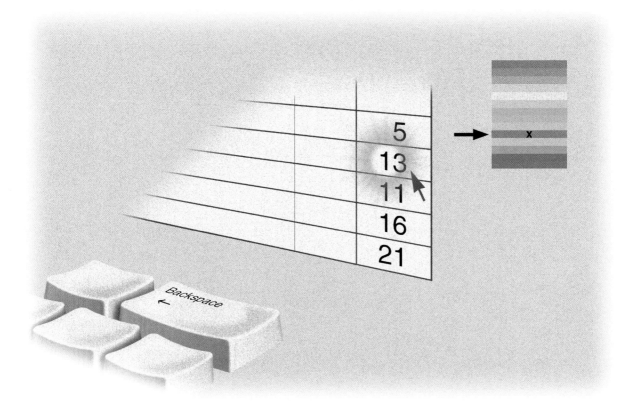

Notice another problem that arises here: The ASCII alphanumeric code maintained by computers doesn't make linguistic judgments. Obviously the book "A History of Newtonian Physics" begins with the letter A followed by a space character; but bookstores generally discard "a," "an," and "the" at the front of book titles, and sort by the next word. For that reason, some libraries choose to list such books like this: "History of Newtonian Physics, A." Regional book warehouses are not libraries, so they don't care nearly as much about the indefinite article. Their electronic lists, therefore, generally place "a," "an," and "the" in front; so when bookstores download the lists, they get the articles up front whether they want them or not. A good application must be capable of weeding them out—or at least sorting for the book in either place on the list.

Finally, above is an example of a user mistake, in which a user realizes that an existing entry is incorrect. A good application should make it easy to make corrections. At the same time, it must be able to translate that correction into its own data tables without the user having to be informed of this internal realignment. If an entry in a cumulative table becomes unsorted, therefore, the application must re-sort it and not say anything about it.

CHAPTER 10

MAKING THE APPLICATION USABLE

Mitch Kapor's "dashboard" analogy—that you can't build a car around its dashboard—makes sense up to a point. The point is, the dashboard—the part of the product from where the user controls its functions—is a make-or-break element in the sale of the product. Even if the car has a great engine, if the controls aren't in the right place or the right order, there's no point in owning it. Suddenly, the "dashboard" architect becomes very important after all.

The user interface—the controls and menus on programs—has changed drastically over the past few years. Whereas modern applications such as the Excel spreadsheet and the Word for Windows word processor are very intuitive mouse-driven programs, the original WordStar word processor had a list of commands and shortcuts that filled the top half of your screen, and the early Lotus 1-2-3 spreadsheets had menus that were nearly impossible to access. Although a programmer still would not think up an idea for a great interface and *then* decide whether this program would be an accounting program or a word processor, the successful programmer of today's Windows-based programs must begin thinking of the interface soon after deciding what the program is for. The most successful applications today have integrated controls built into the design from the initial stages. Still, computer applications are confusing at times. The programmer's objective is not to make the application run as second-nature to the novice programmer, but rather to keep from making the application *unnecessarily* confusing.

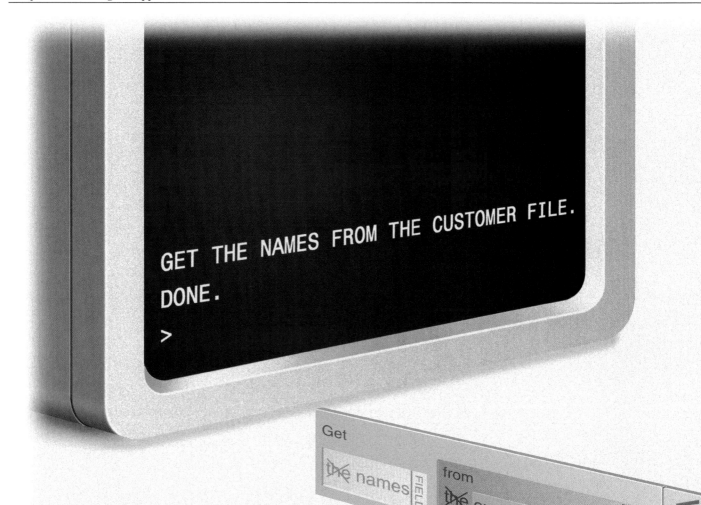

INTERPRETING AN ENGLISH-LANGUAGE COMMAND

Before graphical environments (such as Windows), the most advanced applications were those that interpreted the user's commands from English-like sentences. The more like everyday English the sentences were, the better the program was considered.

A program that interprets English commands might look simple when running, but it is actually very difficult to design and build. When a user types something like GET THE NAMES FROM THE CUSTOMERS FILE, it amazes the amateur onlooker that the computer can respond to something so simply phrased. What the onlooker isn't generally privy to, however, is the rules by which this command was phrased.

The engine that interprets English commands for a computer is called the *parser*. Users have had the most fun with parsers in the "interactive fiction" games distributed by Infocom during the 1970s and 80s, such as Zork. Even today there are no "complete" parsers. Parsers use fixed sentence structures based on the placement of keywords, generally verbs or adjectives such as "how many" and "when." These fixed structures are represented here with templates, with slots where other words can be inserted.

In the sentence command shown here, GET THE NAMES FROM THE CUSTOMERS FILE, GET is the key verb. There might be only one valid sentence structure associated with GET, in which the element to be "gotten" immediately follows GET, and the location from which to retrieve it follows. Articles such as "the" are allowed if only to maintain the illusion that the computer is reading English; the parser generally throws them out.

NAMES is a field or group of fields from the data file that contains names. FROM THE CUSTOMERS FILE is not as sophisticated a phrase as it appears. FROM tells the parser that there is a specific point where NAMES can be found; in some cases, FROM may not even be a necessary term. The only truly important element here is CUSTOMERS; the other words could easily be thrown out. GET, NAMES, and CUSTOMERS are the three most important elements in the command; some parsers would even allow the user to type GET NAMES CUSTOMERS rather than the full sentence.

More sophisticated parsers today use *semantic networks*, similar to electronic thesauruses, to broaden the vocabulary of the program. Semantic networks make it possible for the user to use a wider range of words, and have the parser make the connection between the word the user chose and one that actually means something in the program's command vocabulary.

If you've ever used the thesaurus feature on a modern word processor, you know that you can highlight a word, and the application shows you a list of synonyms for that word. Semantic networks are similar in their composition. Not only do they connect synonyms, but also they contain internal values that represent the degree of correlation between terms.

In the semantic network diagram shown here, "build" and "make" are very closely related, whereas "fry" and "make" are distantly related. The relative "closeness" of words to one another in a semantic network can be counted. By linking synonyms to other synonyms, the semantic network computes a cumulative distance between distantly related words—similar to finding the distance between two cities on a map.

Suppose a program responded to *make* only as a command verb. The user enters *create* instead; should the program respond with a SYNTAX ERROR? Not if the semantic network can equate *create* with *make* beforehand, and replace one for the other. But, of course, this application could still be error-prone, because the application still doesn't "know" the meanings of any of the words—especially when you look at the number of possible definitions of a single word such as *make*.

GRAPHICAL USER INTERACTION AND HOW IT WORKS

The purpose of graphical environments is to make applications simpler to use as well as to explain. If this were truly the purpose of computer development, programmers would have perfected the English language parser long before the graphical environment; why use a mouse, after all, when you can just speak your commands?

The real purpose of the graphical environment is to make data more visible, more tangible, and more widely applicable. IBM is the main force behind the development of a set of doctrines governing graphical

environments in applications, called Common User Access (CUA). Both Windows and OS/2 are based on CUA. IBM has a process for visualizing data and interpreting it as information with CUA.

Imagine that you are writing a program to be used by NASA. Your program must maintain raw data regarding the management and monitoring of a space shuttle. Computers can easily store and retrieve this raw data; but that alone won't make anything easier for anyone at NASA. If it is used for only storage and retrieval, the computer is nothing more than an electronic filing cabinet.

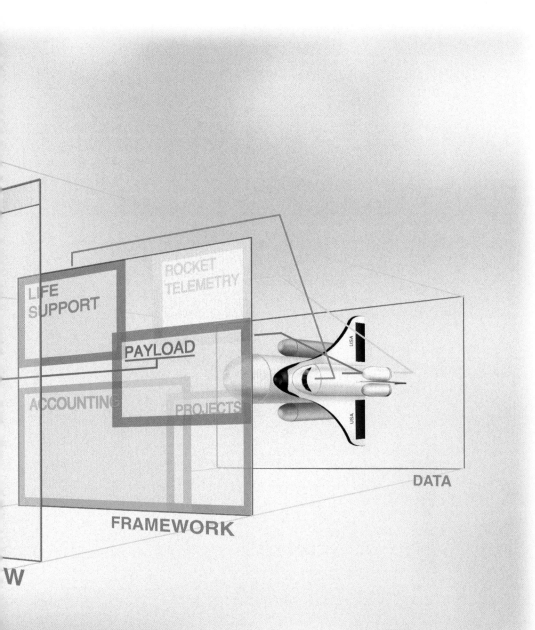

The first step in making data more accessible graphically is to divide that data into separate elements or divisions of data, called *contexts*. Each context may contain a separate data file relative to the database at large. The way these contexts are organized in relation to each other is the *framework*. Some data, such as payload, is vital to all elements of the framework, and is shared among contexts; other contexts, such as accounting and rocket telemetry, are kept separate.

It's then the job of the graphical environment to display the data from these contexts so that it makes sense. The realm of

data might form its own separate toolbar or menu, which it calls a *view*. The combination of these different views into one usable program takes place in the *object* layer. IBM calls data elements "objects" in an attempt to give them surface and tangibility—in other words, to make data into *things* that the user can appear to touch and hold. Associating one element with another, therefore, is easily accomplished with a drag-and-drop operation that requires little or no explanation beforehand.

THE CONVERSATIONAL MODEL

The easiest programs to use ask precisely what you want, make requests for vital information in an understandable manner, and display results that are easily interpretable. In short, the most pleasant applications are the most *conversational*.

This seems to conflict greatly with the graphical models currently in fashion. A conversational model program needs to do little more than ask questions and present an answer. For instance, to calculate the future value of your annuity, it need only ask your present value, your length of term, and your interest rate. It could, conceivably, perform its function over the radio, or through a bank teller booth such as this one. A conversation program has a simple flowchart such as the one at right: ask a question, ask another question, ask another question—display a result.

The user interface for a conversation program is also extremely simple to implement, as shown at upper right. Each set of questions the user will be asked is scripted in advance. The program answers each question with one of the supplied, scripted answers from a main menu. The program takes the user into the script and back out into the menu.

A conversational model program is easiest to program, easiest to implement, and easiest to use. So what's all this hoopla over windows, mice, and objects? First of all, a conversational model program is little more than a calculator. It figures a result without giving the user any more understanding of the original information than would an algebra textbook. Furthermore, such a program is not versatile. The user cannot make it conform to his personal needs because it is not general in nature.

Besides, a word processor cannot be conversational. A conversational model program is not responsive *on its own*; it can only be triggered to use prescribed requests, and even then *it* requests information and work from *you*, rather than the reverse.

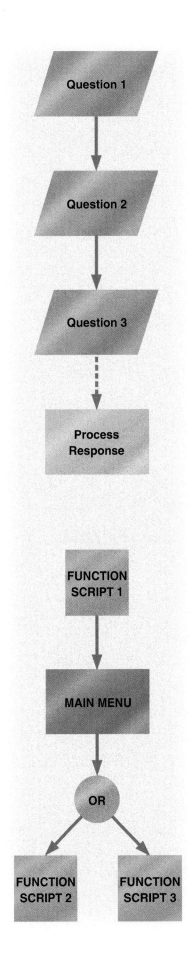

THE EVENT-DRIVEN MODEL

You've seen how modern graphical environments process events; now perhaps you have a better understanding of *why*. A conversational model program is based around a script, whereas an event-driven program is based around *communication*—both between programs and users, and between programs and each other. The event system lets *you* trigger a process, and have the application respond to what *you* request rather than the other way around.

Whether an application is conversational or event-driven in nature doesn't necessarily have a direct bearing on the "engine" processes of the program. You saw in Chapter 9 how program code is engineered and refined; those models would have been the same whether their applications were running off of OS/2 or simply the DOS prompt. What goes on inside the application structure, therefore, is its own business as far as the user is concerned.

The same is the case with this skyscraper. Each office of the skyscraper represents a different option available to the program, but only certain programs are available or active at this time—the offices with the lights on. The rotating clock hand circles around the skyscraper, granting time shares to requesting offices or processes. Each process can choose how to present itself to the outside world (to the user). From the user's point of view, what appears on the outside of the window (the toolbar and dialog box here), makes all the difference.

Is There Such a Thing as a Common User?

A minority of computer applications produced for the public at large are nongraphical. The producers of these applications claim that their models focus on the "common user," named for IBM's Common User Access guidelines for graphical operation.

Some newcomers to computers believe that they can literally ask a computer questions and it will spit out answers like an old-time ticker-tape machine. Event-driven computers prove that communication with a machine is not always best achieved by language alone. Yet some newcomers are easily confused by the alternative to language. Is this confusion really necessary? All that any application truly *does* is accumulate data, reorganize it, and display it in the same or some other form. A word processor is merely a storage system for characters, and a "desktop publishing" program is merely a word processor with graphics. The core engine of these programs can be modeled simply as a data-in/data-out flowchart.

So, couldn't scripts be worked out for these simple exchanges of data in and out of the machine? The Common User Access standard says that scripts are *not* the key to effective communication. CUA is based largely on the ideal that users can describe to the computer what they want by pointing to it, and can convey their data to the computer by fill-

ing the appropriate box the way they would on a tax return. The ideal here is that all communication can be reduced to pointing to menu entries or icons and filling in the appropriate blanks. CUA thus assumes that users can point-and-click on anything they want done; all computing is a data-in/data-out process.

Not so. CUA forgets the principle assumptions and primary needs of new computer users: to convey information with their own native tool, *language*.

If every computing function was operated by point-and-click, computing would be a far more difficult process than it is now. An application must have more efficient means for getting data from the user than mere buttons and switches. If point-and-click was the only medium of communication open to the programmer, it would follow that the more processing power an application is given, the more buttons it would take to access that power. A panel full of hundreds of buttons is more confusing than even a DOS prompt.

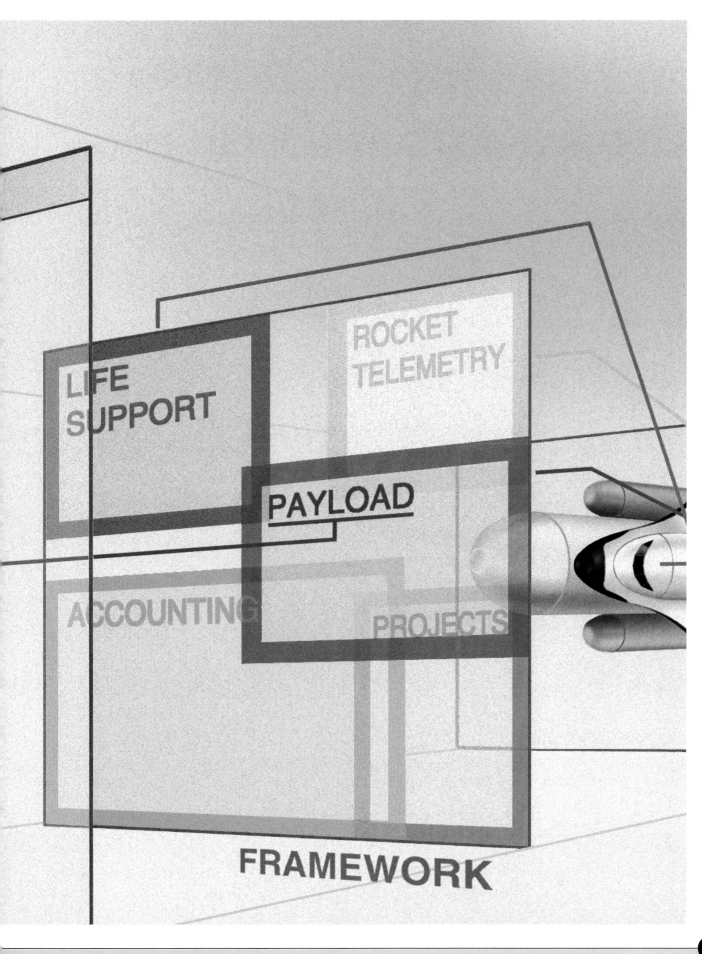

THE GLOBAL USER INTERACTION CONVENTIONS

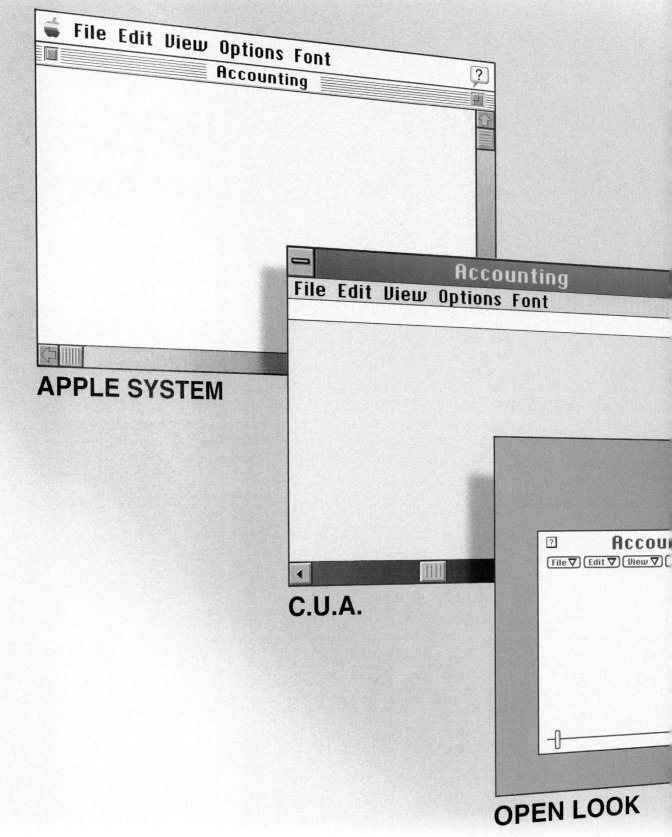

You can make an application more usable by making it closely fit its native environment. Conversely, the program is more marketable when it can be rewritten (*ported*) from one environment to another with as few changes as possible.

The major graphical environments are not very different from one another on the surface. A second glance at an application running on three different platforms shows that every application has its menu bars, its tool icons, and now even its own "how-to" information system. The process model for an application does not need to change much—perhaps not even at all—to support multiple platforms.

What you cannot tell from the surface is that the platforms of the individual operating systems provide the communications between applications and the operating system. In the Apple System, the event structure that links running applications is conversational in nature; a sort of question-and-answer session takes place between programs.

In Common User Access systems such as Windows, Windows NT, and OS/2, the event structure is about as conversational as a bulletin board. Events are given their own terms; then they are "posted" to a stack of such events and retrieved later by the operating system. In the Windows 3.1 CUA system, each application is responsible for "posting" other applications and ensuring that they are given time to run. If the application fails to retrieve the next "posted" note, it fails to execute the next event; it hogs the system and everyone else just has to stand in line.

UNIX-based environments such as Open Look are heavily regulated by the operating system. Events in this and other X Windows environments are functional requests to the operating system, passing data to the OS much like a procedural programming language passes data to its `main()` function. These event requests are submitted and processed, and the results are given back to the application when the function is complete. Each running application has its own direct pipeline to the OS through which messages can be passed. These event messages aren't tokens stating the way things are, as in CUA, but they are function header requests, just as though they were accessing C or C++ functions—and they are.

Writing an application for all three of these platforms allows the programmer to develop a uniform program code, although by all means he would need to write three different user interfaces. There is no other way.

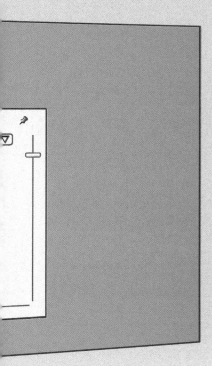

CHAPTER 11

UNDERSTANDING PLATFORMS

It's difficult for anyone to build a new and sustainable industry without a model. The model for the microcomputer industry, some argue, was the automobile industry; although by 1980, four years after microcomputers were officially "born," computing had itself become a model industry.

In the 1970s, however, some people felt that the only way to add more power and functionality to a computer was to redesign the entire computer, the same way a car manufacturer rolls out a new line every two or three years. The original computer was designed with about 4K of RAM, with a screen that could show only four colors. This computer ran BASIC all the time.

It was soon discovered, however, that software—not just hardware—could shape the way people use a computer. You didn't have to run just BASIC. Soon, a program became more than just a function of the computer; it became a new way for people to work. To change the way you worked, you simply changed the software.

The software industry still could not flourish, however, if every time a manufacturer wanted to release a program for another brand of computer, it had to rewrite the software from scratch. The solution to this predicament came by accident rather than by design. IBM couldn't place an absolute patent on the design of its Personal Computer. As a result, other manufacturers could design their own machines to work the same way as IBM's, as long as they didn't use IBM's blueprints to do so. To run IBM's software, however, required IBM's operating system, which was really Microsoft's operating system. By licensing MS-DOS to whomever met its requirements, Microsoft developed what can rightly be considered the first microcomputer platform.

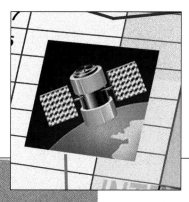

HOW THE OPERATING SYSTEM FACILITATES A PROGRAM

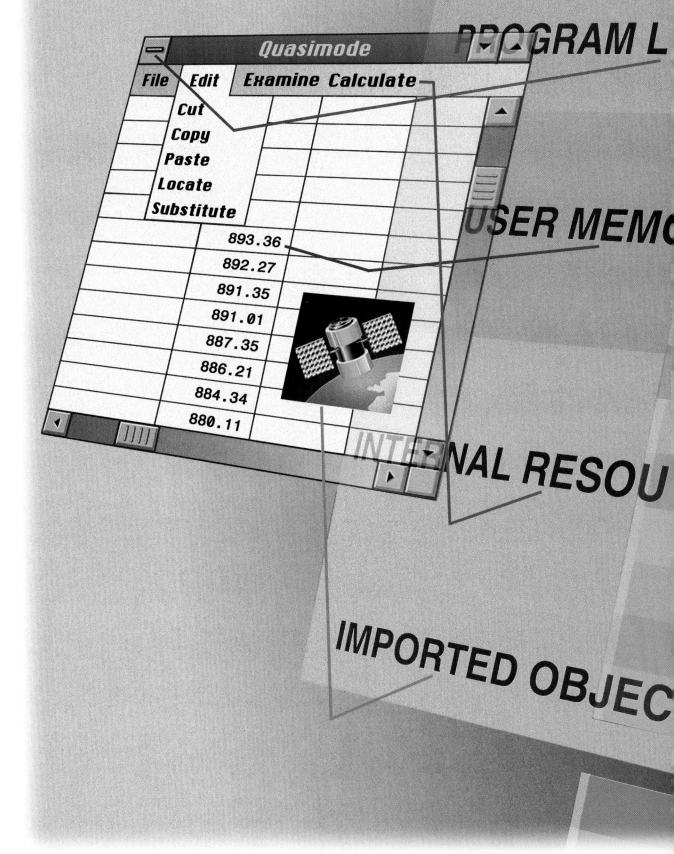

EAP

ATION RAM

I n computing terminology, a platform is a standard combination of an operating system and an operating environment. Examples of common platforms include MS-DOS and Windows, and UNIX and X Windows. Programmers rely on platforms to stay the same even when they're supported by thousands of different computer brands; whether a user is operating a COMPAQ, a Dell, or something his neighbor built in his garage, DOS is DOS. Likewise, two UNIX clients sharing data over a wide-area network may see the same application with two different views—one with Motif and the other with Solaris—although both clients are using the same program in the same way. The platform is the reliable component that provides uniformity in the system, despite the underlying differences in the hardware and the overlaying differences in the environment.

One of the main functions of a platform is to act as a "middleman" between the application and the computer hardware. In a multitasking system, the portions of the computer's memory assigned to any one task are generally scattered throughout the computer's physical memory. The platform's purpose is to convey to the application the "impression" that its own local memory is one contiguous memory slice; an application doesn't need to know, therefore, that its allocation of user memory (represented in purple on this page) is in 60 or so different pieces strewn about the RAM (random-access memory) like an airbrush scatters paint. The application "sees" one unbroken area of memory, because its supporting platform (whether it's Windows, X Windows, or the Apple System) maintains an internal map that links each segment of the application's view of memory to its true location in RAM.

HOW AN ENVIRONMENT PROVIDES GRAPHICAL RESOURCES

You've seen how an operating environment uses and processes events. When you move the mouse pointer, click a button on-screen, or switch from one running task to another, the operating platform (the operating system and environment together) recognizes these as events (remember the red marbles from Chapter 1?). Although there is no one way in which all platforms respond to events, there is one proper way in which the current platform is supposed to respond.

Just what part of the system responds and how depends in large part on how the different components of the application are "wired." Generally, the environment gives an application its own window, complete with the standard frame and controls. When programming in modern platforms, the programmer hardly ever has to manually create these resources for his application; the environment most likely gives him all the resources his application requests.

This sketch shows an ordinary application hoisted to the "ceiling" of a mechanic's garage to show you what goes on under the surface of your application. Now, the environment provides the application with these requested resources, although the environment also maintains them as well. The application can be triggered to respond to events associated with the window gadgets—for instance, moving a window to the front, minimizing it to an icon, moving one of the scroll bars—but the environment also responds to these events, regardless of whether the application does anything. In other words, resources provided by the platform are wired to that platform.

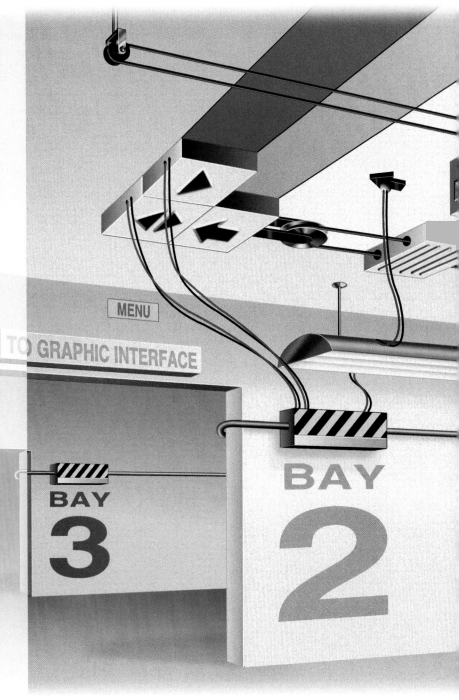

MENU

TO GRAPHIC INTERFACE

BAY 3

BAY 2

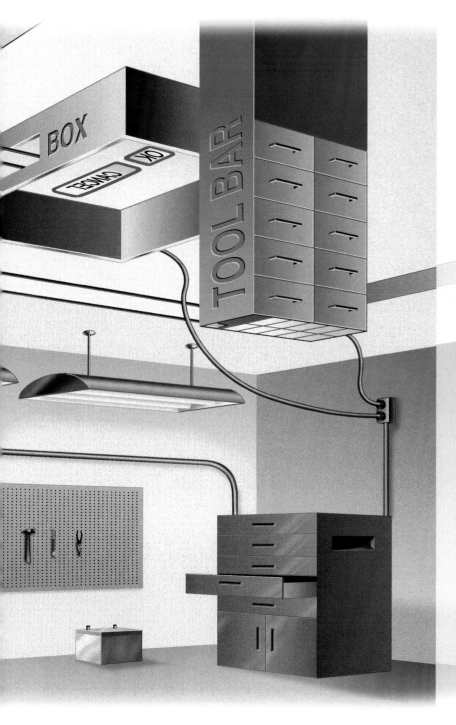

Notice that all of the standard platform objects (such as the scroll bars, minimize and maximize buttons, and mouse pointer) are wired to the platform's yellow event queue box on the wall. Depending on the platform, this event queue can be handled as a stack of events to be processed when the system gets around to it, or as a constant pipeline of direct function calls to the system. The events in the queue are processed in the order in which they're received—one way or the other—by the platform's graphics interface. This is the component of the system that connects the resources to the kernel—the platform's "engine."

At times, the platform gives responsibility for some of the ordinary platform functions, such as dialog panels and toolbars, to the application. This means the application alone produces the buttons and gadgets necessary for these devices to appear on-screen and be functional. Rather than design the mechanisms for these components from scratch, programmers can rely on the application framework—pre-designed components that behave as dialog panels and toolbars. This framework—represented here by the red toolbox in the corner of the garage—is provided not by any part of the platform, but by the interpreter/compiler package the programmer chooses to use or purchase separately. Most C++ compilers have their own tool libraries full of ready-to-use dialog panels; all the programmer needs to do is write the code to access one. Likewise, to make a toolbar work, the programmer need only give it icons for its buttons and links to the parts of the application they will activate.

PLANNING FOR PLATFORM INDEPENDENCE

T he fact that more than one computing platform exists today is evidence that there is no one way computers work. Software manufacturers demand that their programmers craft their applications so that they support more than one platform. At the same time, they demand that each version of the application support as many facets and special features of that platform as possible.

This demand is perhaps impossible to fulfill. Designing an application for multiple platforms is, as you'd expect, like finding the least common denominator in a set of fractions; or, as this diagram suggests, determining where the platforms overlap. Certainly only a small subset of the features of an application could be supported by every platform. Yet how many features in this subset are supported by all the platforms in the same way? Perhaps none.

This leads to one of the greatest dilemmas facing programmers today: how to design for multiple platforms simultaneously. The solution some programmers have been attempting is to write the core engine of their application—the axis, represented here by the flagpole at center—in a generic form of C or C++, without including any function calls specific to one platform. Instead, when an application needs to perform a function that the platforms each handle differently, the axis places a call or a branch to another module outside of the axis—"in orbit." This module is named the same for each version of the application—for instance, `slide_window()`. Yet the contents of the "orbital" modules are designed differently for each platform, so that they can be tailored without disrupting the core functionality of the axis.

The Portability Problem

The first microcomputer operating system to appear to work the same way on all computers, regardless of the brand of computer being used, was called CP/M (Control Program for Microcomputers). Designed by Digital Research Inc. (now part of Novell), CP/M used the same general command vocabulary on each computer it supported.

The problem with CP/M, however, was that it had no supporting platform beneath it. As a result, whenever a new brand of computer came along, CP/M had to be rewritten from scratch to support it. DRI worked frantically to constantly reconstruct its operating system for each new computer on the market.

The reason MS-DOS became far more popular than CP/M had less to do with CP/M's functionality (which was actually quite elegant for its time) than the fact that Microsoft had far less work to do to make MS-DOS universal than did DRI. The design of the IBM Personal Computer divided the "control program" into two components: the operating system (OS) and Basic Input/Output System (BIOS). MS-DOS handled the operating system components (those that processed and interpreted the user input) and managed the location of files on the disk. The BIOS was separated from the operating

system, and it extracted the character-by-character input from the computer hardware. Manufacturers still had to rewrite the BIOS each time the hardware was redesigned; but the "hooks" to the BIOS were kept uniform with each redesign, so the operating system could literally stay the same.

CP/M, on the other hand, was designed to do both jobs—communicating with the hardware and the user. Originally, this was a big selling point for CP/M; but eventually, it became the system's downfall. The microcomputer industry was created, for all intents and purposes, when it was decided that the components that should change should be separated from the components that should stay the same. The changing components would act as the platform for the uniform components. This way, the user wouldn't notice any difference from system to system, and there could be a more universal way to use computers.

Rather than a thousand or so separate platforms today—as there could have been had this layering principle not been discovered—there are just a handful. It therefore seems logical, from the software marketers' point of view, that an application can be written to support all these platforms, because there are so few. The problem with this idea has to do with the vast differences in system engineering between these platforms.

The Common User Access platform (which includes Windows and OS/2) relies for the most part on processor architecture designed by Intel. There are other brands of processors that work in place of Intel's, such as Cyrix's competitive line; on the whole, however, CUA is supported by the Intel design. It doesn't really make sense on the surface that a way to point an arrow at a button is rooted to the way a CPU handles logic gates and transistors. In computing, however, the two concepts are directly linked, despite the many layers of architecture that link them.

The Apple System relies on processor architecture designed by Motorola. Recently, IBM and Motorola teamed with Apple to design a new architecture called PowerPC that will support the Apple System, among others. Still, Apple's software is linked to Motorola's hardware. UNIX and its X environment, by stark contrast, is designed not to support any one processor design in particular. X and the CPU are separated by several layers

of subordinate platforms, so you can run X on an Intel, on a Motorola, and on a National Semiconductor CPU and not notice any differences on the surface.

The portability problem, therefore, involves both the marketing and design divisions of a software manufacturer—and it stumps them both. Every operating platform has its "specific elements" (for example, QuickTime and Object Linking and Embedding) and the platform manufacturers ask their software developers to support these elements, or else not receive support from the platform manufacturer in their corporate advertising and promotions. Supporting these specific elements means that the application's architecture must be divided into unrelated versions; in turn, some things are done the same and others aren't.

WHAT ONLY ONE PLATFORM CAN PROVIDE

N ot every application ever conceived has to support all the operating platforms. Manufacturers have seized on some categories that capitalize on the differences between platforms and highlight specific features of a specific platform. Often marketing leads a manufacturer to choose only one popular platform and concentrate its energies there.

Some software manufacturers have found their fortune in platform-specific utilities, such as programs that monitor and enhance the performance of the environment. No computer user hasn't at some time run out of memory or system resources—regardless of what he's got on the machine. One example of a platform-specific utility is a package such as PC Tools or Norton Utilities. Because utility packages work on hardware and operating systems, they are necessarily more platform-specific. A user could not fine-tune his system if the utility package was portable. This nonportability also makes the package more marketable; a more effective product sells better, and therefore produces more money.

Until recent times, only supercomputers could be measured in terms of Millions of Instructions Per Second (MIPS). Now the fastest PCs are measured in terms of MIPS. The only applications that can run fast enough on a PC to be measured in MIPS must be platform-specific; platform-generic applications must spend too much time reading and translating code and instructions.

By designing an application to run on only one platform, the programmer can take advantage of the features of that platform, without having to divide modules between axis components and orbital components. As a result, the application can be smaller and faster. An application written in assembly language is generally faster than one written in compiled C or C++, perhaps because humans are better at designing shortcuts and tighter code than are automated systems. A compiler writes the machine-language executable code based on the more understandable high-level language code the programmer gives it. By cutting out the middleman, the assembly

language programmer is free to design tighter code, tailoring it along the way to fit the key design elements of a specific CPU, whether it is an Intel or a Motorola. Because the operating system and environment are so closely tied together, handwritten Assembler code makes the most of this closeness.

One other popular category of platform-specific software is the type designed to enhance the operability of the environment, making the user more comfortable while tying more higher-level graphical functions to the operating system. Some manufacturers call this category *enhanced desktops*, borrowing from the analogy that a computer screen is like the surface of a desk. A company can design several such desktops for several platforms that are each used in the same or similar manner; by nature, their underlying engines must, however, be radically different. Most enhanced desktops attempt to rearrange the environment so that it looks more like a Macintosh, which has been acclaimed as one of the better designed "desktops." You can think of this in terms of the tourist telescope shown on the facing page; when the application is defined for only one plane (or platform), there are no irrelevant objects from adjacent planes sticking up in the way. The application can "see" further, and therefore has more insight into the terrain of the application.

WHEN THE HARDWARE CHANGES THE SOFTWARE

The nonaxis elements of a portable application are defined by the differences in the components of computers. On Intel-based computer systems, the predominant platform for video display is called VGA (Video Graphics Array). It isn't the only video platform, but it's the major one. Still, there are about three dozen ways a video card can supply VGA to the system; as a result, many programmers have to write specific video drivers so that their software is supported on differently configured video displays.

On Apple computers, there is only one way to produce sound—as defined by the hardware of the Macintosh. Apple programmers have no problem, therefore, making their applications make noise. Other platforms don't have this luxury, because their computer's basic architecture is supplied only with a beeper. How sound is produced, therefore, is sometimes dependent on how the user configures the software, forcing the programmer to give the user multiple possible configurations.

Users of telecommunications software have less trouble hooking up their modems and dialing a major service or a bulletin board. Programmers of telecommunications software, however, are faced with a nightmare of international standards written in barely translatable languages, which are amended and changed almost weekly.

With the popularity of Graphical User Interface platforms, such as Windows and X Windows, relatively few programmers still need to directly access the BIOS of a computer. DOS programmers, however, must still access the BIOS to perform memory checks and position the cursor, among other things. Diagnostic software, however, must be intimately familiar with all the types of BIOS currently available for a CPU's different architectures.

The CPU is the root element that defines how a computer system works. Most operating platforms are designed around how a CPU works. How much a platform is tied to a CPU is directly related to the degree in which machine language was used in the platform's design. UNIX was designed to never require a specific CPU, so its

designers always assumed that its components would be written in the C language. On the opposite end of the scale, the first designers of the Apple System not only assumed their platform would require a Motorola 68000-series CPU, but also would always be run in a Macintosh. Microsoft Windows was originally designed around the Intel CPU architecture, but successive versions of Windows rely less on Intel. As a result, one version (Windows NT) currently exists for Digital Equipment's Alpha CPU.

When an application supports a CPU, must it support its associated optional math-coprocessors as well? An Intel 486 CPU has math coprocessing built into the chip itself; however, separate coprocessors are still available. To make an application universal, you could leave out coprocessor support; but doing so may sacrifice some of the special capability of the 486. Most applications now include software emulators that activate if there is no math coprocessor.

Memory, for the sake of nearly every component of the computer but the BIOS, is memory. From the hardware's point of view, there are two main memory architectures, DRAM and SIMM. The software doesn't care about this, and therefore neither does the programmer. What does matter to the programmer is how much memory there is. Most operating environments require two megabytes of RAM just to run; but because they're environments, there should be some RAM left over. It always makes sense to make an application as memory-conservative as possible; however, a database manager is faster and more effective if it can allocate more RAM for itself, for use in searches and swaps. If that RAM is unavailable, the database manager must run more slowly; when timing is critical to an application, slow data access can be unacceptable.

CHAPTER 12

THE TEST BED

As a publishing company, every year you produce hundreds of new book titles that teach you how to construct a computer program. Some of your books use flowcharting, whereas others simply point out the features and nuances of the terms in a programming language. In this chapter, you learn how to conceive a program.

Conceiving a program is certainly a worthy feat. But it's practically a law that programs, no matter how well conceived, will not run correctly on the first go-round. As you have seen throughout this book, a program is a combination of intricate modules designed to function together as a whole. Although these routines or modules are a simple concept on paper, when combined with thousands of others, you can't expect them to fit together perfectly immediately.

All programming is a trial-and-error process. It's not that programmers don't know what they're doing; on the contrary, they know too well that their task is all about trying again.

The most well-written programs are those first planned on paper before the actual writing or coding ever begins. This allows the programmers to anticipate many problems and incorrect logic before the application is half-written. Many programmers begin writing code before they have thought through the concept and completed the design, and thus end up with ill-designed and poorly structured code nearly impossible to maintain—which must often be completely rewritten rather than updated. The programmer also breaks down complex ideas into simple concepts, then quickly produces carefully tailored prototypes—just as an engineer would with a new mechanical device.

The way a programmer can tell right away whether his routines are functioning properly is the same way a user can tell: The result isn't what it's supposed to be. A routine or module, as

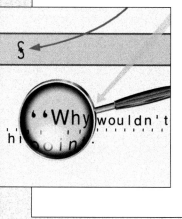

you've seen, is a machine that moves data from the input to the output and changes it along the way. When the data comes out wrong, it's almost impossible for anyone to tell by looking at the surface of the program why that happened. It's supposed to be impossible; most good applications shield their users from the intricacies of their operation.

NOW THE HARD PART: HOW TESTING WORKS

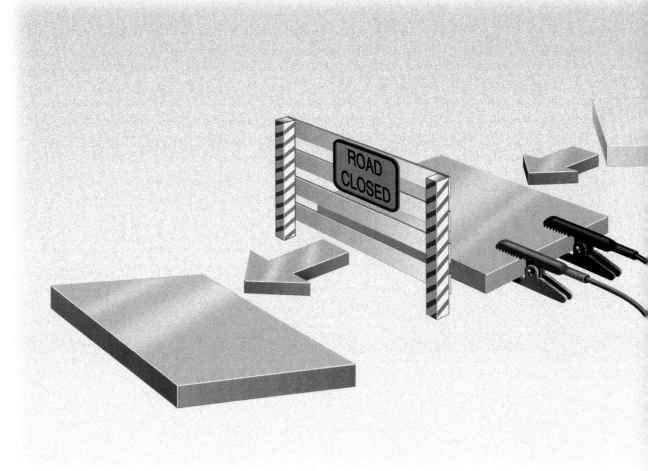

To see what's going on, a programmer has to slow his routine and monitor its progress with a special type of program, often called a *debugger*. A debugger program allows the programmer to run the program in a controlled state, at a slower, highly exposed setting. The values of any or all of the routine's internal variables are displayed to the screen at all times. Maps of memory are shown, detailing which memory blocks the routine is accessing.

Among the tools a debugger program uses is something called a *breakpoint*. It acts as a gate that halts execution of the routine and enables the programmer to look at the program variables and memory. If the routine is looking at the wrong place in memory for its values, or some address in the right location in memory is being set to the wrong value, the programmer can see that at the breakpoint.

From the breakpoint, the programmer has the option of slowing the execution speed, or single-stepping through the instructions in the source code, pressing a function key to activate each instruction. This way, the programmer can monitor the "footsteps" of the routine—like watching a film frame-by-frame to see if you missed part of the action.

A good debugger program also allows the programmer to alter the execution path of the routine manually, first by establishing "roadblocks" that prevent some routines from being called until they have been debugged. Many debuggers also allow the programmer to actually simulate error conditions in case the routine is not in error, in order to test the error-trapping and corrective features of the program.

ANATOMY OF A BUG

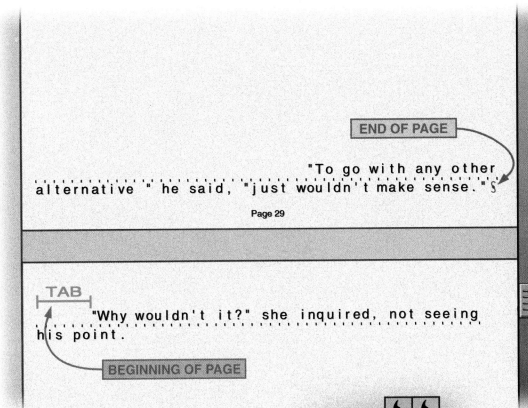

A bug, on the other hand, is an incorrect instruction, but not an invalid instruction, that causes the program to produce valid results, but not the desired results. The program does the wrong thing, but the computer can't know that.

What does a bug really look like? In this example, it looks like an entire page of missing text. Here's how a bug might come about: Suppose that the programmer has modeled the data in his word processor so that the "Top of Page" and the "Bottom of Page" are both marked by individual characters that the user doesn't see. The illustration above diagrams a page break, and shows where these invisible signal characters are located.

One of the ordinary functions a modern word processor performs is to correct one of the inadequacies of the old typewriter keyboard: In typesetting, there are two quotation marks, one for the beginning of a quote and one for the end. On many

computer keyboards, there's only one key for the quotation mark, just to the left of the carriage return on the home row. Normally, the character produced with this key looks like two marks pointing straight down; but the smart word processor we are designing will change these marks automatically to appear as two separate quotation marks curved properly around the quotation to represent an open or closed quote. In most cases, one character is automatically converted to two.

Here's how a simple correction becomes a catastrophe: A word processor application isn't accustomed to seeing the number of characters in a document increase without

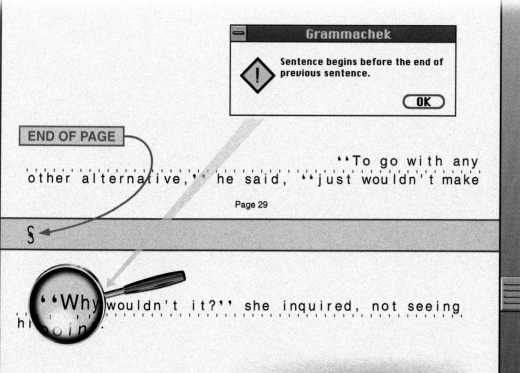

the user having added those characters. Suppose, as the panel at top right shows, using two characters to represent open and closed quotes causes one of the words on a line to wrap down to the next line. This pushes the other words in the paragraph down one line and, unless the word processor knows what's going on, pushes the "End of Page" indicator far below the end of the page. This could, theoretically, put text that continues to exist in the computer's memory in an invisible location below the bottom of the page.

You can't expect a grammar checker to look for invisible text. So assume that the grammar checker part of the application is running on automatic, and it hops over the accidentally placed invisible text. It then notices a sentence on the next page with an open-quote and a capitalized word—it appears that a new sentence begins before the prior one ends. Using the rules of punctuation, the grammar checker then removes the open quote (which it thinks is an error) and lowercases the first word on the page. Next, it might have the word processor

move what was the first word of that sentence so that it follows the last word of the prior sentence—which exists in that invisible realm that was created accidentally. Now the "End of Page" and "Beginning of Page" are both off the page, forcing a countless number of characters to enter what many programmers actually do call the "twilight zone."

AN ERROR VERSUS A BUG: SETTING TRAPS

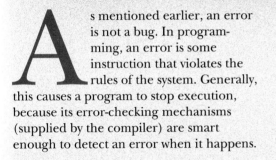

As mentioned earlier, an error is not a bug. In programming, an error is some instruction that violates the rules of the system. Generally, this causes a program to stop execution, because its error-checking mechanisms (supplied by the compiler) are smart enough to detect an error when it happens.

In BASIC, the ON ERROR GOTO instruction has the computer keep an eye open for a pending error condition. Like GOTO, this is a branch instruction; but it's really a branch waiting to happen. After ON ERROR GOTO is executed, the program goes about its business. After an error occurs, the program

In some systems, this creates an error condition; but again, it's a good error. It tells the application not to bother trying to plot this part of the drawing if the user isn't supposed to be seeing it, anyway.

Another error common to low-level language and to C programming occurs when a value being held in memory starts to exceed the number of binary digits allocated for it. For instance, an eight-bit positive integer (whole number) can be equal to any value between 0 and 255 ($2^8 - 1$); but suppose a routine attempts to add a number to this value where the sum is greater than 255. This creates an overflow

immediately branches to the instruction label that immediately follows the GOTO part of the instruction—regardless of the fact that the ON ERROR part was executed a long time ago.

One of the strangest things about errors is that a program that works properly does contain error conditions. In fact, a well-written application actually expects errors to occur. One of the most commonly expected errors is a "not-found" condition, such as a File Not Found or Record Not Found. Before adding a record to a database, a routine may search for a record that contains the same or similar contents to the one being added. If such a record isn't found, that's an error condition, but it's really one you want. The routine is then free to add the record; otherwise, it should notify you that such a record already exists.

Another frequent type of error is the "out-of-bounds" condition, especially with regard to graphics. In most applications, you can't move your mouse pointer beyond the boundaries of the screen. When the pointer is at the edge of the screen, a conditional clause tells a routine not to update the pointer location along the axis of that edge. If the application is the one doing the drawing, however, at certain window magnifications some of the graphics being drawn may overlap the boundaries of the screen.

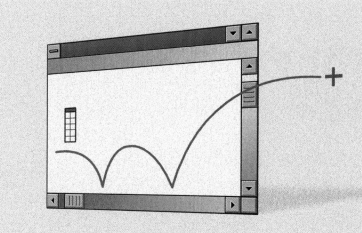

condition, which may set the Overflow flag in the CPU's status register. Such an error may or may not be "good"; a routine may allocate another variable or address for this value with a greater number of bits and relocate it there, or it may choose to disallow the addition altogether for some reason.

Why a Programmer Wants Things to Fail

A veteran programmer knows that "development" and "debugging" are practically synonymous. At the point where planning, flowcharting, and modeling ends, debugging begins.

As you saw in the preceding pages, placing an error in your program can be good; but usually only if it is a planned error that is intentionally placed in the code. Even a well-planned, well-placed error, however, can cease to be good if it is not removed. If an application ships to a hundred thousand customers, and there's an error somewhere in the code, the error ceases to be good. Errors in a program are trappable within the program; rather than have the computer tell the programmer there's an error, stop execution, and exit the program, he may instead have it say there's an error, have it stop execution where it is, and let the programmer examine it. He may also write a trap routine using ON ERROR GOTO (or the equivalent in some other language) which tells the program to determine for itself what the error is and take its own corrective measures.

An "error," psychologically speaking, is actually a misunderstanding. If the file for which a routine is looking is not found, if an

algorithm attempts to divide a value by zero, or if an algorithm attempts to add the value 6 to the word "hypoglycemia," the program generates an error condition that the programmer could have easily avoided. On the other hand, if a routine searches for a file name on the active storage device and it isn't found, that too generates an error, although it can be used as an intentional error. The programmer actually plans his routine around the potential occurrence of that error.

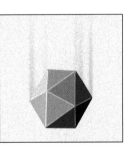

According to the definition subscribed to by professional programmers, a bug is a far more serious matter than an error. The bugged program may go about its business after the bug is encountered, regardless of how far astray the program has gone. This is why the debugger program is necessary to slow things down. Rather than make things better automatically—as the name "debugger" seems to imply—such a program makes it possible for the programmer to watch things get worse from a closer vantage point.

A bug is a situation in which the normal course of the program is thrown off track, and neither the computer nor the programmer knows why at first. The application might proceed along its normal course of execution, although its

memory pointers may be off, its flag variables may be flagging something else entirely, and its text fields may start to contain happy faces and up-arrow characters rather than the names and phone numbers the programmer intended them to contain. No programmer can trap a bug. She can prevent it from occurring, or she can rid her program of it after it's discovered, but she cannot have her program anticipate it automatically. Contrary to popular thinking, the more skilled the programmer becomes, the bigger her programs will be. As the program becomes more complex, proportionately more bugs are generated. But as she gains more experience, she will learn to recognize and remove these bugs more quickly.

HOW USERS AID THE CONSTRUCTION PROCESS

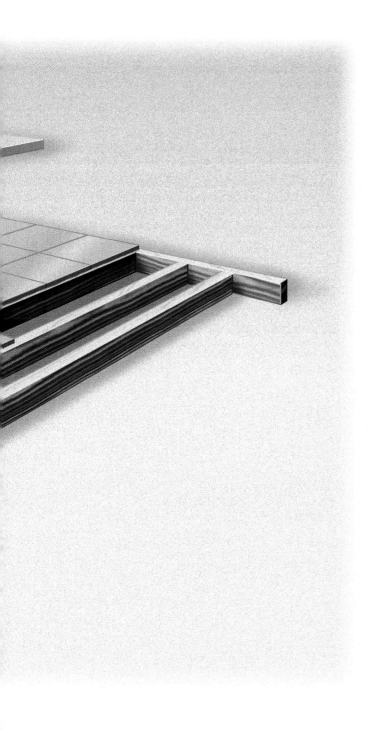

A major software manufacturer may employ dozens of programmers to develop different aspects and facets of one application. Despite their multitude, such programmers—regardless of their qualifications—often can't see their own mistakes.

Furthermore, the work environment of a programmer is generally not at all like that of a stockbroker, an accountant, a mechanical engineer, a surgeon, or a meteorologist. These people are more concerned with their everyday tasks than they are with how to operate a computer. They want the computer to work for them, rather than the other way around. A programmer may only have an opinion of how these people work, based on any number of interviews and on-site inspections; but most likely, he doesn't share the same experiences as these people. As a result, when a programmer is writing an application for people outside his work environment, he may not be able to test the program as well as these professionals can.

There is an entirely new type of job that could only have been born in the 20th century: the beta tester. This person is the programmer's "copy editor." The term "beta tester" comes from the "beta" name given an application deemed not ready for public release. Not only does a beta tester use a beta program rigorously and report all problems he finds, he also gives the programmer new insight as to what an ordinary person does in his everyday work environment, and how the application can best be tailored to fit that environment.

Beta testing often begins before many areas of the program are completed.

WHEN CLIENTS DEFINE THE APPLICATION

Many people sometimes assume that all programmers work for a large corporation such as Microsoft or Borland, when in fact many programmers today work for themselves. Rather than write for millions of potential users, they write for about five or six. These particular programmers encounter problems that the corporate programmers are shielded from—including answering directly to their users.

What the programmer-for-hire learns quickly in his business is that no application he writes will ever truly be done. The comment, "It's perfect; we love every aspect of the program; you're truly a miracle-worker" is heard only in this person's dreams.

Because of this, the programmer actually structures his application differently to accommodate changes that might take place at some future date. A new employee in the office may bring with him some new skill that he wishes the office application would facilitate. The application, therefore, needs not only to be modular, but also open-ended so that the programmer can add these features without undermining or altogether destroying his work so far.

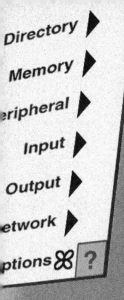

Directory ▶
Memory ▶
eripheral ▶
Input ▶
Output ▶
etwork ▶
ptions ⌘ ?

TYPESETTI	Ie
	Co
	Fu
	Op

OVERV

Better Results

DATA ACCESS

Object	▶
Item	▶
Edit	▶
Locate	⌘
Define	□
Add	⊡
Delete	□
Form	□
Rotation	)▶
Query	>▶
Calculate	□
Project	▶
Function	⊡
Text	□
Options	⌘ ?

CHAPTER 13

THE NEXT COMPUTER APPLICATIONS

One of the nice things about authors in the field of computing is that they get to be historians in a relatively short period of time. In 1976, authors wrote about how to use a computer. You learned about the various switches and levers you needed to press and hold, about the little LEDs you had to watch, and how best to interpret the readings from your paper tape in a shorter time.

In 1978, when you turned on your computer and there was BASIC, you learned how to use a computer. You learned about preplanning your line numbers, about numbering your subroutines so that the numbers didn't conflict with each other, and about the type of etiquette you should use when having your program prompt its user for input. In 1984, you started over again with how to use a computer. You learned how to keep your floppy disks in order, what this new "application" thing means, how you enter a program, how you exit a program, and how you determine the best subdirectory structure for saving files.

When 1990 came along, you had to start playing catch-up. Rather than type commands, you clicked on them. The button for calling up a certain function showed up on your screen rather than on your keyboard.

Now it's 1994 and you're still behind. Computing authors become historians because, by the time they got through telling you what tomorrow on your computer would be like, it's already yesterday's news. Today is a world of objects, of structured queries, and of user-customizable toolbars. Commands have been replaced by options, and syntax errors with gentle warnings. You add something from one form to another form by picking it up and moving it there.

Yet it's all about to change again. The future of computing is all about being able to learn (and comprehend) new technology quickly. You comprehend the computer, and the computer comprehends you in turn. You'd think all this would be accomplished by making operating the computer look and feel more like working in the real world.

Not really.

THE META-APPLICATION CONCEPT

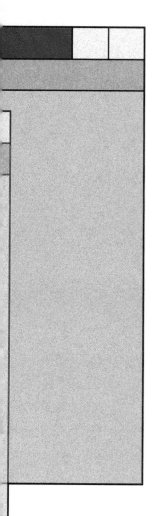

Because of the way computers once worked, users grew accustomed to going *into* applications and exiting *out* of them, as well as going into and out of subdirectories. This is an old model—a throwback to when computers could run only one application at a time.

When you think of multitasking, generally you see a bunch of task windows inhabiting the screen at one time, each with its own document contained within it. This user interface, too, is seen as a throwback; you're still exiting one and entering the other, even though you're looking at them both at the same time.

What will change about this user interface is its inherent redundancy. When the operating system or platform gives each application a standardized *object* view of its own data, each application will be looking at the same data. It will no longer be necessary, then, for the data in those applications to be contained in multiple copies in each of those applications. The *functions* of those applications will remain separate, although the user will see only one copy of the data, or one document. Every major operating system designer is working to develop this concept, called in some circles the *meta-application.*

Designing an application around the meta-application ideal will radically alter the way you program. In a sense, rather than having "Windows," you'll just have a "window." From the programmer's perspective, the user's view of the data will be provided not by the application (such as Lotus 1-2-3), but by the operating system (such as Windows or UNIX). All the application needs to provide is the *functionality*, along with the "hooks" to the operating system's projection of the data.

This could make applications *smaller,* because much of their code is currently spent displaying their own data within their own windows. Furthermore, programmers will spend less time and effort designing the *format* of their data, allowing them to devote more time to the *arrangement* of that data. The role of applications in a meta-application environment would be to provide added functionality toward the data maintained by the operating system.

NEW FORMS OF USER INPUT

I t is amazing what new forms of input devices are being conjured up in computing laboratories. Some people choose to attribute these new devices to research in "virtual reality"; the simplicity and everyday familiarity of these devices are so ingenious that they are perhaps attributable instead to "real reality."

Take, for instance, this incredible new device called the *microphone*, which is now being tested to see whether it can be used to get input directly from a user's voice. By means of sophisticated artificial intelligence algorithms, the sound waves created by the voice patterns can be matched against a known set of words in the application, in order to recognize words and form commands. Semantic networks, as we saw in Chapter 10, can then be used to decipher the meanings of these patterns, so that computers can one day accept commands from ordinary spoken language.

One of the most complex pointing devices ever created is the *finger*. Hardware engineers are taking advantage of this amazing device by placing electrostatic fields along the surfaces of computer displays, thus creating *touch-screens*. This way, the user can select a command simply by touching a button on-screen. The field sensors detect where the finger pressed the screen, and the program converts these readings into screen coordinates. These coordinates are just as good as those used to plot the location of the mouse pointer. These touch-sensitive screens are in use at libraries throughout the country for electronic card-catalog systems.

Finally, a simple and elegant input device used today on smaller and smaller computers is the *pencil.* Users of hand-held computers are now able to write their commands and information on a line on the computer's display. Again, the points where the pencil presses the screen are converted to screen coordinates, thus allowing the user to write data directly to the screen. Algorithms are then used to analyze the shapes of the marks made, to convert them into letters, digits, or single-stroke commands shaped like proofreading marks. Also known as *pen computing,* this technology has been presented by several companies at computer trade shows for several years now.

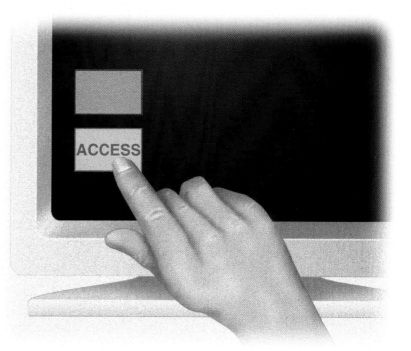

DOCUMENT-CENTRICITY

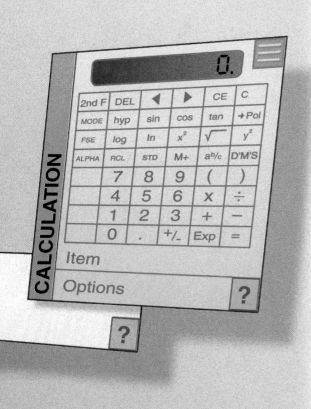

The key to making the new meta-application concept work, and making new users *accept* it, is an idea some developers call *the document-centric model.* Computers and operating systems so far have been *application-centric*, meaning that they are mostly concerned with running applications and not with the underlying data.

The document-centric model takes the focus away from the application; in fact, it could just make the computer application so open-ended that it is almost invisible. The user of a new document-centric system may one day find himself purchasing *functions* rather than applications. These functions would then be grouped together by the operating system in individual panels; all functions pertaining to word processing, for instance, would be grouped in one panel. These functions may be provided by different software manufacturers—the contents of the "Function" menu under the "Typesetting" category, for instance, may be produced by one company, whereas those of the "Edit" menu may be produced by another.

The document-centric model would allow the user to select specifically those functions that he needs to perform his job, and install those into his operating system. Those functions he does *not* need can easily be left out; and the specialized functions that perhaps only he and a few dozen others in this world would ever want would be as much a part of his computer environment as those parts that everyone uses all the time.

THE NEW OPERATING SYSTEMS

As you learned in "An Understanding of Platforms," a computing system is made more versatile when it is *layered*—especially when one layer provides services to another. Today, an operating environment provides windowing resources and graphics devices to its applications; this way, the programmer doesn't have to write code that defines a scroll bar, menu bar, and pointer. These things are assumed to be already present in the system. This is an example of a device interface layer providing services to the user application layer.

Future operating systems such as those being designed by IBM, Microsoft, AT&T, Apple, NeXT, and Taligent (an IBM/Apple joint venture) all provide greater functionality by employing *more layers*. This diagram shows the layers in the new systems *above* the base layer of the operating system.

Key to the design of future operating systems is the capability for them to run applications designed for *other operating systems*. A *virtual machine* is literally a simulated computer and operating system within an operating system that has been given the impression that it has the computer all to itself. You'll see more about the implications of this development in the next few pages.

All operating systems and subsystems in the new designs provide services to the *object management facilities*, the handlers for user-created data in the new document-centric model. In this model, the responsibility for accessing, displaying, and storing data is shifted from the application to the operating system. The applications themselves are provided their own data using the same types of function calls by which they are given their own windows and menu bars today. This is why the Primary Task layer is placed above the Object Management layer in this diagram.

Future operating systems will be far more capable of allowing the user to define and even design new functions for his applications. This doesn't mean every user will have to become skilled in BASIC or some other high-level language. It means that the application will have more space and time to give its users more tools—especially by way of spoken language input—for concocting new functions for their personalized applications. The system that allows the applications to give this new duty to the users will also be a part of the new operating systems—at the User-Defined Process layer.

HOW THE SUBSYSTEM WILL CHANGE EVERYTHING

The assumption that there is *one* way to perform any computing task will be thrown out when these new operating systems are installed on all your machines. Every user will be given a choice of ways to do things. The way that works for a particular user will be made to work on his computer.

This leads to the importance of this new computing device called the *subsystem*. This device will allow each user to run *virtual machine* programs within his operating system, which in turn allow programs written for another operating system to run on his machine. An MS-DOS virtual machine program currently runs within Microsoft's Windows NT operating system. Sixteen-bit versions of Windows 3.x are themselves contained by the DOS operating system; in the NT scheme, DOS is contained within Windows. Whereas each DOS session has its own device drivers and its own local 640K block of conventional memory, Windows 3.1 applications also have their own virtual machine—with each Windows 3.1 application operating off of the same virtual machine.

Operating systems in the near future will be capable of running Apple Finder subsystems within an OS/2 host, and vice versa. An application written for Windows could then be run on a Macintosh, any other Apple machine, or any machine licensed to use Apple's technology. Furthermore, software manufacturers could develop their own subsystems with features and functions specifically designed for a certain work category—such as manufacturing, astronomy, or warehousing. It would be as though a major operating system existed for *just that very purpose*; users will be able to install these subsystems in their computers as easily as they install a shrink-wrapped application today.

This situation means that the user's view of the computing world—shown here—will change significantly. No longer will one person's computer be an island unto itself, or one local-area network a string of tiny islands in an endless ocean of data.

In Closing

Programming began in the 1940s as a labor of setting switches and dials and replacing blown-out vacuum tubes. In a half century, it has become an art form, another means of human expression.

Throughout the 20th century, the office workplace has drastically changed. The proper posture for operating the typewriter was developed and taught; today, businesses use portable computers with keyboards designed to be held on people's laps. The codes of conduct and etiquette taught for formal communication between employees and officers of the company often fall to the wayside with the use of electronic mail. We write happy faces to each other at the end of E-mail notes with an eight, a dash, and a closed parenthesis.

The computer industry was created when industry-wide standards were first used and accepted by all software manufacturers. When there were at last just a handful of major operating systems rather than several hundred small ones, building a software industry became feasible. Computing engineers began dividing the services of a computer into neat, regulated layers; and then they devised standardized interfaces for one layer to provide resources and services to the next.

When the operating system services became more standardized and regulated, the programmer became more free to create and devise new concepts for operation, such as the window itself, and the spreadsheet-inspired, event-driven user interface. The software industry flourished because the operating systems became reliable.

Up to this point, however, users have had to deal with the steep learning curve of integrating the computer into their everyday life. A user has his choice of three or four major brands of spreadsheets and word processors; and as far as the software sales industry is concerned, those are enough choices. The everyday user, however, is more ingenious than his software. He wants to be able to not only "customize" his applications—to add little icons here and there and change the color of the menu bar—but also to devise new ways to work, to optimize his computing environment and that of his company. The user will, to some extent, become the programmer.

People do not want to succumb to a way of working devised and programmed by someone else. They would much rather see the computer conform to the way *they* work. That's why this book was written. As a computer user, you—like it or not—are now a programmer. You will not begin writing your own word processor or spreadsheet applications any time soon, but you do have the background needed to begin writing your own programs and applications. And that seems to be the future trend in the office and computing—you can do anything you choose.

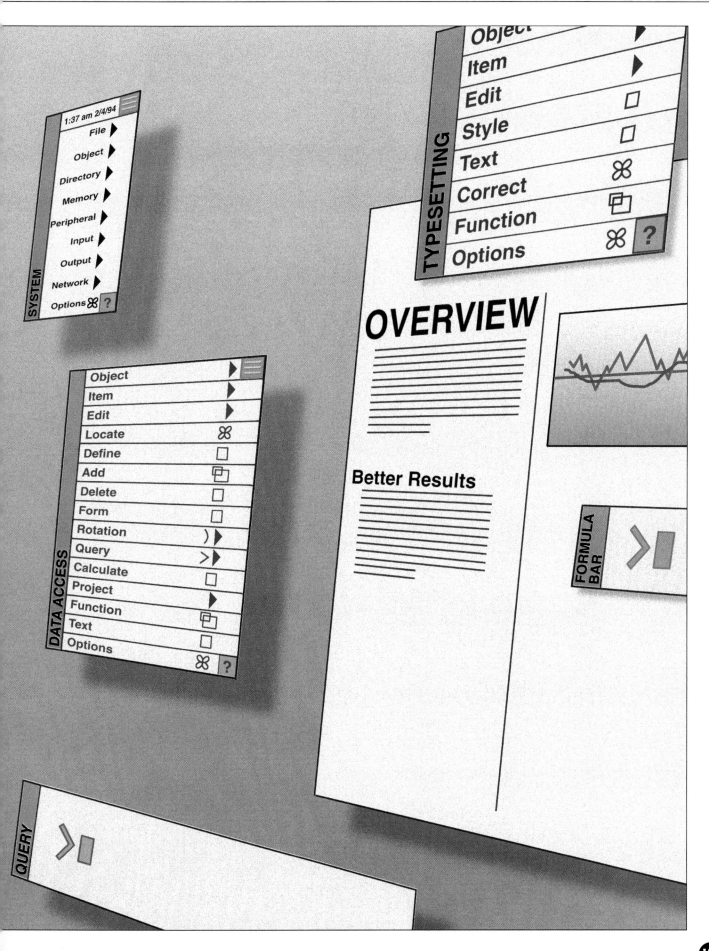

INDEX

E

editors, 20-21
end product, 108-109
engines (applications), 112-113
enhanced desktops, 155
errors
    bug comparison, 164-165
    trapping, 165-167
event-driven programs, 138-139
exclusive-OR, 65
expressions, 49

F

fetches (flowcharts), 105
fingers, 176
flags, binary values as, 54-55
flowcharts, 104-105, 113
formatting data, 75, 80
FORTRAN, 30
fourth-generation languages, 31
frameworks, 135
functions
    BASIC, 94-95
    SUM( ), 85

G

gates, 65
global variables, 96
goto instruction, 43
graphical
    applications, 25
        CUA standard, 134-135,
            140-141, 143
    environments, 148-149
    objects, 57
graphics
    programs, 6
    VGA (video graphics adapters), 156
GW-BASIC, 94

H

handshaking, 115
headers (files), 22-23, 44, 80-81
hexadecimal math, 62
high-level languages, 11, 30-31, 89-101
    BASIC, 94-95
    C, 98-99
    COBOL, 93, 100-101
    PASCAL, 96-97
    structures, 89
Hopper, Grace (Rear Admiral), 93

I–K

IBM PC, 152
    development, 145
If instruction, 41
IF statements, 104
IF-THEN comparisons, 85
indexing databases, 72-73, 125
input
    parameters, 23
    users
        fingers, 176
        microphone-based input, 176
        pen computing, 177
        touch screens, 176
instructions, 36
    BASIC, 94
    branch, 43
    goto, 43
    If, 41
    nested, 38
integers, 44
inter-application communications, 122-123
inter-program dialog, 114-115
interpreters, 20-21, 27
interpreting commands, 132-133
iteration, 39

Kapor, Mitch (Lotus Development Corp.),
    119, 123, 131
Kemeny, John G., 95
keywords, 37
Kurtz, Thomas, 95

L

M

N–O